THROUGH TRIALS TO GLORY

THROUGH TRIALS TO GLORY

*The Life and Trials of Loraine
and Richard Kelly*

Loraine Kelly

Library of Congress Control Number: 2015918159
ISBN: Hardcover   978-1-5144-2291-5
                   Softcover   978-1-5144-2290-8
                   eBook   978-1-5144-2289-2

Print information available on the last page.

Rev. date: 11/11/2015

To order additional copies of this book, contact:
Xlibris
1-888-795-4274
www.Xlibris.com
Orders@Xlibris.com
727264

CONTENTS

For my children
Sherri and John

and my grandchildren
Georgia, Ellie, Edward, Harry, Paige and Kalan

for all the ways they brighten my life

INTRODUCTION

History would be an excellent
thing, if only it were true.

—Leo Tolstoy

Much has been written about Richard Kelly's life and career—and mine. It has been said that "the human brain is hard-wired for narrative—stories are everywhere, told by people, for people, and about people." Because the facts have been altered in other publications to support the government's case and to accomplish a political agenda, I feel the need to tell my story about the trials we endured and set the record straight.

If I do not write about my life as the wife of Richard Kelly and try to make sense of the trials, and about survival after it all fell apart for my children, grandchildren, and children after them, tomorrow will be like yesterday; it will not be done—the time is now.

Growing up in Brunswick and the tranquil picturesque Golden Isles of Georgia in a comfortable middle-class Baptist family sheltered my life more than I realized until that day in April 1960, when I married Richard Kelly for the second time. This was just weeks after he qualified to run for the office of Circuit Judge in the Sixth Judicial Circuit of Florida (Pasco and Pinellas Counties). I had married a barefoot boy from a foster home who understood the problems in his home county and who was brave enough to tackle these issues and chart his course to do something about them. When I became his partner, I was thrust into the public arena much like a lamb being released into a lion's den. I was ill prepared for what was to follow.

1

ADOLESCENCE AND EDUCATION

To what end am I destined?

Unlike my stable childhood, my husband's was chaotic and dysfunctional. Kelly's father was a civil engineer with the State Department who never lived with his mother during his lifetime. Kelly spent some of his early years in a Rhode Island orphanage and with a grandmother in Clearwater, Florida, before returning briefly to live with his mother in St. Petersburg when he was about nine years old. He was taken away from his mother and placed in a series of foster homes after government regulations put his mother out of her homemade candy business. The business collapse caused his mother to start drinking again and forced him to go to work delivering papers and taking a series of other jobs that ultimately led him to quit school. His departure from school led state officials to have him placed in the foster home in Zephyrhills.

Richard Kelly grew up in Pasco County, Florida, and was educated in its public schools. During World War II, he served in the U.S. Marine Corps, Second Marine Division, in the Central Pacific. With help from the GI Bill, Kelly worked his way through Colorado State College of Education, majoring in government and education where he earned varsity letters in two sports: football and tennis. After graduation, Kelly taught government and coached football and basketball in a western Colorado high school for a short time before attending Vanderbilt College of Law; he eventually returned to Florida and the University of Florida College of Law where he earned a law degree.

Kelly served as an associate of W. Kenneth Barnes, former judge of the Court of Records in Pasco County, for five months. In 1953, he opened a law office in Zephyrhills and later became the senior partner in the firm of Kelly & Bales. Kelly was serving for the second time as attorney for the City of Zephyrhills when he received the appointment as a federal prosecutor. He also acted as attorney for the FBI and represented the U.S. government before the U.S. Court of Appeals in New Orleans, and he qualified to practice before the U.S. Supreme Court.

In his job as U.S. attorney, Kelly gained valuable court experience in preparation for the run for the circuit judgeship in Pasco County. He came to know and understand the politics of his home county, saw the bad being done to good people, and realized the need for someone with courage and the qualifications to take on solving the problems of corruption that existed. He charted his course and prepared himself to take on the "establishment," also referred to as the *clique*.

2

BACKGROUND

The conditions that led to the control of a clique

To understand the politics of Pasco County, Florida, it is important to examine the conditions that led to the wealth and power settling into the hands of a few prominent families. To a large measure, these families consisted of the Auvils, the Covingtons, the Daytons, and the Larkins. Exactly how these families amassed their wealth was largely a matter of speculation. The old-timers of the county had a lot of stories to tell.

Almost without exception, the controlling families of the county either had connections with Pasco Packing Company, which was the largest employer in the county, or were members of the Bar. A dynasty composed of these few families developed at the expense of the workers and the economics of the area.

By the late 1930s and early 1940s, the transfer of power from the older overlords to the younger generation had begun. Of primary concern in this new generation were two sets of brothers—E. B. and Sid Larkin and George and Orville Dayton. The younger generation concentrated itself almost entirely in the law profession. The dynasty took on the form of a clique or otherwise known as the establishment. This clique dabbled in other areas with the more progressive and wealthier plunging headlong into increasing their power and wealth. The Larkins, in particular, soon owned great amounts of land and cattle. The members of the clique, both directly and indirectly, controlled many jobs and a great percentage of the area's wealth.

The clique, though not present in a corporal body, controlled the government of the county to the extent where one almost needed their approval to run for office, and surely their approval was needed in order to win an election. Many offices in the Pasco County courthouse were filled with either family members or their puppets. These puppets in no way went against the desires of the clique. Thus the numbers of the clique increased by the number of the puppets, and the power increased accordingly.

With the situation of a growing clique with ever-increasing power, one could wonder why the people did not revolt and order a change. The answer was in the fact that the clique operated on human weakness. Because the clique was some fifty or more years in the making, the awesomeness of it was never fully realized by the greater majority of the people. By the time the average person did realize the situation, the feeling was that it was useless to fight the clique. Elections consisted almost entirely of unopposed incumbents with only a few lesser offices drawing opposition. The people felt that the elections were cut and dried long before Election Day, and therefore, they stayed away from the polls in droves. This lack of voting strength was exactly what the clique needed to thrive and grow. The people lacked both the drive and leadership to fight back against the odds.

In 1957, Pasco County had a population of about thirty-six thousand people. The average per capita income was $1,129, compared to the state average of $1,775, as per *Florida Reference Atlas*.

This was compounded by the fact that every county immediately surrounding Pasco had a higher per capita income at the same time. This not only placed Pasco below the state average but also made it an island of despair in a sea of wealth.

The main source of income was from the cattle and citrus industries, with some 84 percent of the land being used for farms and citrus. Thus the county was made up—for the most part—of agriculture and workers of related industries, with incomes below the average for both the state and surrounding areas. This condition was even more exaggerated prior to 1957. This situation of hard work and lack of money led to the development of a class of people who had little time for, and even less interest in civic and governmental affairs. These conditions made it quite easy for a person or a group to take over and gain control.

With almost every office in the courthouse being held by another family member or by a puppet, in order to run against the circuit judge, one had to run against all: the clique or the establishment. All were Democrats, as most were in the south, and the county was run by the few families. This was nepotism at its best. It was commonly believed that "you can't beat the bunch in the courthouse."

3

THE ESTABLISHMENT

A patriot must always be ready
to defend his country . . .

—Edward Abbey

The first challenge to the establishment occurred when the *Zephyrhills News* pronounced on February 24, 1956, "Kelly Named as Assistant U.S. Attorney":

> Richard Kelly, 31-year-old Zephyrhills attorney, has received appointment as assistant United States district attorney for the Southern District of Florida, Tampa Division . . .
>
> Friends of Mr. Kelly regard his appointment as recognition of his legal ability. The position is one much coveted by attorneys interested in public life, and similar appointments

seldom are given to one as young as he is. Only two Pasco County men previously have been recognized by federal appointments.

While serving as a federal prosecutor, Kelly successfully prosecuted a Dade City attorney, Gene Auvil, who was a member of the clique by birthright. This attorney was the son-in-law of the county sheriff who also placed high in the clique. Auvil was convicted of misappropriating Veterans Administration funds and was sentenced to a term in prison and was disbarred. This conviction upset the clique beyond measure. Here was one of their members snatched from among them by a young lawyer Kelly, who had been reared in Pasco County and should have known better.

Kelly further increased the number of his enemies by prosecuting several moonshine cases which involved families of long residence in Pasco County. One of the largest bootleg rings in the state of Florida existed in the Zephyrhills area for years. One case involved twenty-five defendants, the seizure of thirty-five trucks and cars, fifteen distilleries, one hundred thirty government witnesses, and many other defendants and vehicles in other related substantive cases. These stills were discovered by state rather than county agents. The irony of it was that it was common knowledge that this was the way these families made their living.

While a federal prosecutor, Kelly also investigated, tried and convicted a Dade City store operator who had sold narcotics illegally over the counter for years.

Although these cases received much publicity, and the members of the clique were upset, Kelly still had not completely awakened the politically sleeping public of the county. They had been controlled and had been without hope for far too long.

In 1960, the awakening began for the first time for many when Kelly resigned as senior United States district attorney for the Southern District in Miami and returned home to run for the resident judgeship of Pasco County, Sixth Judicial Circuit, on the Republican ticket. This in itself was a notable feat for there had never been a resident Republican office holder in the history of Pasco County. Kelly's opponent for this office was incumbent judge Orville Dayton of the historic Dayton family, and a birthright member of the clique. Orville Dayton and his father had held this office for more than sixty-five years. It was commonly known then that if one had a case before the circuit court, one must hire the judge's brother, and the case would pretty much be decided beforehand at the Crest Restaurant across the street from the courthouse. The brother in his overalls and muddy boots, right from the pasture, would then take your case before the court with his brother presiding, and payment could well be your home.

4

THE JOURNEY BEGINS

I have chosen my path and am content with it

Richard Kelly and I had married only three months after our meeting in 1955. I had waited for the right person and believed in my heart that he was the one and only one for me. This marriage was not made public, an idea not well received by me or my family. He convinced me that keeping this information out of the public arena was the best choice at the time. Kelly had work to do in preparing himself for the job ahead. I believed he wanted me on hold and ready when needed and did not want to risk losing me.

In 1960, Kelly qualified to run for the judgeship one week and came to publicly marry me the next. You can imagine what my mother had to say about that. My mother insisted that he return to Florida, choose a church home, and prepare a place for us to live.

Kelly returned to Florida and renovated the small tenant house on his orange grove. This was to become affectionately known by the children as "The Little House" in the grove. The plan was to live on the grove until after the election which would determine where we would ultimately live. Because the political battles kept coming, we lived there for nine years before moving to Holiday on the west side of the county.

Because my family was Baptist, Kelly first went to the Zephyrhills Baptist minister to talk about his faith and a church home for us. The minister questioned his intentions and political motivations, and that was the end of that. Kelly was better received at the Dade City Presbyterian Church where we became members.

Kelly and I were a part of a small group from Zephyrhills attending the Dade City church wanting to build a church in Zephyrhills where we lived.

The First Presbyterian Church, Zephyrhills, Florida, was founded October 14, 1962. Kelly and I were charter members and were active in the church with our children. Our son, John, was the first to be christened in our new church by Reverend James Frank Merrin, our first pastor.

Kelly served as a trustee and an elder. He was chosen to serve as a commissioner to the 111th General Assembly of the Presbyterian Church in the U.S., which was held at Massanetta Springs,

Virginia. I was told that a hat and gloves would be the appropriate dress for me attending the assembly. As it often happened, my role became secretary for Kelly. The debate was intense, but we experienced that one can disagree in love. Kelly also served as a member of the Presbyterian Judicial Commission, Synod of Florida.

Wanting to know more about how Presbyterians differed from Baptists, I took advantage of every training opportunity; later I even served as district chairman, Women of the Church, Westminster Presbytery for Leadership and Resources. My responsibilities were to train women in leadership positions and supply the resources needed to seven churches in the district.

After the home was ready and the church chosen, Kelly then returned two weeks later for our wedding at the First Baptist Church, Brunswick, Georgia, on April 24, 1960. The time between marriages was filled with college and work, and a stronger union was formed.

Going into Kelly's home area as the wife of the candidate, and especially a Republican candidate in a Democratic world, was not easy.

More than half disliked me, and I was labeled the villain even before meeting the first person. Kelly's best advice for me when we got married was that I alone was responsible for keeping myself happy. If help were not coming from Kelly, then from where would it come? "Thy word is a lamp unto my feet, and a light unto my path." My path had been chosen.

5

JUDGESHIP

The impossible realized

To support ourselves, a law office of Kelly & Howay was opened across the street from the courthouse. Julian Howay was fresh out of law school and became a good partner, supporter, and friend. I served as the secretary, made the drapes, furnished the office, did probate work, processed SBA loans, and campaigned, not to mention all involved in being just married. Remember, no help in keeping me happy!

Since few would openly pledge their support for Kelly, my assuming (or marrying) the responsibility of organizing the campaign and the candidate came by default. My approach was from ignorance, but this too served us well. This for me was Politics 101. Identifying boundaries of the Sixth Judicial Circuit and locating more than three hundred Pinellas and Pasco Republican executive

THROUGH TRIALS TO GLORY

committee members was only the beginning. No other candidate had ever undertaken this task. I contacted every available person, arranged every appointment for Kelly, and then was his driver, seeing as many committee members a day as possible. These contacts gave him the opportunity to personally explain the importance of his candidacy and to ask for their help in electing the first resident Republican in the history of Pasco County. We needed as many helpers as we could find.

Pasco County was grouped with the Republican stronghold of Pinellas County to form the Sixth Judicial Circuit. That was a lot of ground to cover.

The unbelievable happened. All of the hard work by many had paid off. Kelly made local political history in November 1960, when he was elected to the Pasco bench as a Republican in a solidly Democratic County. He carried Pinellas County and with it won a close decision over Dayton. Nobody expected Kelly to win, but out of a quarter of a million votes, he won by 420. Although Kelly failed to carry the election in Pasco County, it is very important to note that he did receive 43.5 percent of the county votes even though only 17 percent of the voters were registered Republican.

Now the clique was really worried. Their archenemy—a Republican enemy at that— was about to be seated in an office of high importance within the county. They also realized that here was a man they would not be able to control, for it was obvious that Judge Kelly would not be a puppet judge. The clique would no longer be able to conduct business as usual.

A measure of the power held by the clique can only explain the then-governor Collins reappointing the man Kelly had just defeated. This was the first of several "This can't be done—but it happened!" actions to follow. This angered many because this happened even before Judge Kelly had taken office. The law stated: "One judge for every fifty thousand people." Pasco County was entitled to only one judge; now we had two. Kelly remained the resident judge; therefore, Dayton's appointment did not have the importance or clout he wanted. Having two judges in Pasco County necessitated our being in Pinellas County every other week, even though Kelly was the duly elected resident judge.

Any account of Richard Kelly's life must include his passion for hunting, fishing, camping, or tennis—anything outdoors. He loved sports but not as a spectator.

After winning the judgeship in November of 1960, rather than celebrating at home, we were off to the mountains of Colorado big game hunting. This became a pattern every year of our married life. This year was different in that it was late in the hunting season, thus subjecting us to weather much too cold.

Our destination this trip was Steamboat Mesa, high in the mountains, and the road so narrow that checking on the passenger's side to be sure the road was wide enough to allow our camper to keep circling the mountain to the top was critical to our safety. Looking over the side seemed a bottomless pit. It was hard to appreciate the beauty of it all when it was so life threatening.

We set up camp and built a fire. My wool socks collected ice on the front of them while the backs scorched as I tried to keep warm.

The next morning Kelly was off hunting while I was still organizing our camp and camper in the best way possible to survive the bitter cold. It seemed safe enough to pull the camp stove just inside the camper so that preparing our meals would be a bit more comfortable. Over time I was to learn that it was not a good idea.

Several days passed, and I was not feeling well, but I carried on until Kelly tried to awaken me one night and could not. We were very much alone on top of the mountain. We had seen no other hunters. Kelly had been affected as well, as evidenced by his leaving the camper only dressed in his long johns. It was our good fortune that hunters were poaching nearby that night and saw Kelly wandering in his underwear. They thought him crazy and wanted nothing to do with him. He convinced the hunters that he needed help in getting off the mountain by asking them to check the camper. They found me unconscious.

We were taken down the mountain to a crossroads makeshift trailer cafe set up for hunters next to a filling station. Kelly got out of our camper that had been driven by one of the hunters and went into the trailer cafe still in his underwear and ordered a glass of milk. He was asked, "What about your wife?" His condition was such that he had forgotten me. He returned to the camper, put me across his shoulders like a bag of potatoes, and carried me into the trailer. A doctor had been called, and I was revived with oxygen from the filling station. Carbon monoxide poisoning from pulling the stove inside the camper had been my problem. The doctor suggested a motel for me for a few days while Kelly went back hunting.

We returned home to adjust to the expected changes that would come from the successful campaign. The minor unusual health concerns that I was experiencing were thought to be from the carbon monoxide poisoning. Kelly was even holding my feet while I did sit-ups to get rid of the tummy. Almost three months went by before going to the doctor for a checkup. Much to my surprise, I was pregnant. This was my first, and I believed all was going well.

Dr. Brownlee and my husband had kept from me that there were only five cases at the time of carbon monoxide poisoning during the first trimester of the pregnancy, and four of the five already born had birth defects. Kelly was so on edge, and this explains why he insisted on having a dinner party the night Sherri was born. Miracles do happen.

The day Kelly was robed in January of 1961 in the courthouse in Clearwater, a woman came to him afterward and asked to speak with him privately. Kelly asked if I would give him a little time, and we would meet in an hour in the lobby of the hotel next door. An hour passed, and he appeared visibly shaken when he returned, asking for a little more time. He said that the woman had told him that she was his mother, and he needed more time to determine if this were true. Kelly also wanted my permission for her to come live with us if she were who she professed to be. He learned that she had been living in St. Petersburg on welfare for forty years and therefore would have known his whereabouts through the media. She never contacted him. Kelly's mother did want assistance but did not want to live with us. Politically, this could have been a double-edged sword. Who would have understood why he had not been taking care of his mother? It would not have been known that she had abandoned him as a child.

Kelly asked if I would look into how we could help. I went to Welfare and explained our situation. Their directive was, given her advanced age and years on welfare, it would not be advisable to change her living arrangement. We, with the children, visited her and took care of her needs until her death.

Two children, Sherri and John, were born in the Dade City hospital in 1961 and 1962. Sherri was born in Pasco County, and the second week of her life was in Pinellas County. This was before disposable diapers. It took a truck to carry diaper pail, sterilizer, and much more. Our home away from home was the Jolly Roger Motel, St. Petersburg Beach. Even with all the chaos, we have happy memories. The children at an early age learned to swim in the pool there. Sherri's reward for swimming across the pool was a Barbie doll—her choice. John, testing us, jumped off the diving board in his diapers and looked up from the bottom of the pool smiling while proud parents watched in case help was needed. This must have contributed to their being good swimmers today.

6

THE TRIALS BEGIN

Make the lie big . . . keep saying it, and
eventually they will believe it.

—Adolf Hitler

Our orange grove froze the winter of 1961, a foreshadowing of the year that lay ahead. Efforts began to surface about changing the Sixth Judicial Circuit with the sole "purpose of removing Kelly from Pasco County, as the law would require, and send him back to Pinellas County where all those bad Republicans were."

We also learned that a plan for impeachment was already in place even before the election, just in case Kelly was elected, and it was needed. I didn't even know what impeachment meant.

On April 2, 1963, Representative Tommy Stevens announced in Tallahassee that efforts might be made to impeach Judge Kelly. By April 18, he had partially reversed his field, as was consistent with his nature. A Tallahassee newspaper reported Stevens having said that he had only word of mouth evidence and would not start proceedings until he had written proof. However, on May 3, he did introduce a resolution to the House of Representatives calling for the appointment of a seven-man committee to investigate "the alleged misconduct of Judge Kelly."

At the close of the session of the House of Representatives that same day, the Speaker of the House, Mallory Horne, announced the appointment of Representatives Mitchell of Leon County, Russell of Pinellas, Jones of Bay, Arrington of Gadsden, Boyd of Manatee, Griffin of Osceola, and Crews of Baker to the committee to study the situation.

The committee at first refused to allow Judge Kelly to hear the testimony received during the investigation against him but later reversed itself.

Now the saga began to turn. More than fifty witnesses were called by the committee. Judge Kelly's lawyers managed to make a farce out of most of the testimony given. No sworn testimony was required. If one were listening outside the chamber, the sounds from within were much like a Saturday children's matinee.

A brief account of some of the testimony follows:

Joe McClain, a Dade City attorney and former state representative, admitted he had heard lawyers tell Kelly that he had done a good job. His complaint was that Kelly forced him to wear one of his (Kelly's) old coats on an occasion when he appeared before the court in a sport shirt.

Even Johnny Carson asked on his *Late Night Show*, "Have any of you heard of the judge in Florida being impeached because he required lawyers to wear coats in his courtroom?"

Stanley Burnside, clerk of the circuit court, said Judge Kelly ordered him to "cease and desist" when Burnside referred to Judge Kelly's proceedings on the bench as a "performance." Burnside complained that he was called to the courtroom the next day and was "eaten out" by Judge Kelly. Burnside also testified at length on the judgeship campaign.

Zephyrhills City Judge McGavern, called as a witness, said that he had an occasion to check Judge Kelly's record and that even George Dayton had conceded to him that he had gotten fair treatment from Judge Kelly.

Senior judge John U. Byrd of the Sixth Judicial Circuit said he had only one "run in" with Judge Kelly, and this was over who would try criminal cases in Pasco. He stated that Judge Kelly was within his "constitutional rights" in their disagreement. Judge Byrd was the senior judge and was not giving up his usual practice easily.

Circuit court prosecuting attorney Clair Davis complained only that Judge Kelly's trials were too long. He was forced to admit that he had only tried one case before him.

Dade City attorney Charlie Luckie's only specific charge was that Judge Kelly had sent an armed deputy to force him to a court-ordered meeting. Luckie stressed the fact that the deputy was armed. In reality, the deputy was merely delivering a signed order, and all deputies in the county were armed. Luckie also testified at length about the campaign between Dayton and Kelly.

Judge Kelly's court reporter, Jim Swain, complained about Judge Kelly but later had to admit that he had given money to Judge Dayton's 1960 campaign.

Pinellas Circuit Court clerk Avery Gilkerson said that on September 3, 1961, there were 165 cases on appeal, fifty-two of them more than twenty years old. Judge Kelly went to work, and the appeals docket was soon cut to forty-one cases.

Tampa attorney, James Thompson, also a registered Democrat, said that he had given $100 to the Dayton campaign fund, but he had tried three cases before Judge Kelly. Even though he lost all three, Thompson had nothing but praise for him. (Kelly later married Claire, Thompson's ex-wife.)

Robert Rees, a New Port Richey attorney, also a Democrat, said "There is more revenge on the part of the lawyers than on Judge Kelly. The lawyers are angry because Judge Kelly prosecuted Gene Auvil."

In spite of the reversal on the part of many of the supposed prosecution witnesses and such trivial testimony and evidence, the committee of seven ruled on May 29 that the House of Representatives would vote to impeach Judge Kelly.

This move surely surprised the people of Pasco County and the whole state for that matter. When one considers that only four Florida officials prior to Judge Kelly had ever had impeachment proceedings brought against them, and none of these were ever convicted, it didn't seem possible that such a serious action could be levied on the basis of such absurd testimony.

Now the pressure was on. The Speaker of the House called our room in the Tallahassee hotel where we were staying and said he was coming over to offer a deal.

The editor of our local paper, the *Zephyrhills News*, and his wife had ridden to Tallahassee with us for the impeachment proceeding. When we received the call, I left the room to find the Wickstroms. Arrangements were quickly made for the editor and his wife to be in the room next to ours so that they could listen through the key hole to the deal offered. As I was leaving the Wickstroms, I came face to face with the speaker's three representatives as they were getting off the elevator going to our room. I remember being surprised at not seeing the speaker and thinking that the three looked like hoods. In fact, they were Gene Rossi and two other familiar faces from Pasco County. Then I realized that they were also puppets. They looked very uncomfortable at seeing me. It had been written that "A group of persons, whose identity has never been released, visited Judge Kelly in his hotel room in Tallahassee with a compromise." If Judge Kelly would just move out of the county, the charges would not come before the House was the deal offered.

Speaker Horne was so certain that Judge Kelly would accept the deal that he announced to the press that the matter would not come before that session of the legislature due to a lack of time. Horne was also quoted as saying, "The formation of a special investigating committee to act between sessions gives me a small club to hold over his head. Maybe that will make him a little more humble."

Judge Kelly refused the compromise. The *Zephyrhills News* won a prize for their reporting of this trial.

On Friday, May 31, 1963, at 10:08 A.M., Speaker Horne asked for a vote to place the impeachment matter on the calendar for Tuesday, June 4, 1963.

The House was then read the articles of impeachment. But before this matter was put to a vote, a surprise move was made by Speaker Horne, Stevens, and Chappell. They introduced an amendment providing for a committee to be formed to study a new method to remove members of the judiciary. It also made allowance by which any lawyer who had testified against said judge on matters of impeachment might have the judge excused from all their cases before him.

This surprise amendment might be interpreted as indication that Horne and Stevens felt the case against Judge Kelly was too weak to try for impeachment, and they were covering their hides. The amendment failed.

Sworn testimony is not required in the House of Representative; even so, Kelly won. The vote was seventy-two for Kelly and forty-seven against.

Judge Kelly was apparently free. He met with reporters and was quoted as saying, "The situation in Pasco County has been controlled by a few people, and they still want control. It was their way of life, but their way is over."

On the morning of June 5, 1963, Representative Woodie Liles of Hillsborough County and former city attorney for Zephyrhills, who had just the previous day voted against impeachment, rocked the entire State of Florida when he introduced a resolution asking that the resolution to impeach Judge Kelly be reconsidered. The measure passed, and the articles were reread. With little further discussion, the House voted eighty-eight to twenty-nine to impeach.

True to form, on the drive home from Tallahassee, we turned on the car radio to hear the news that the House had gone back into session and reversed itself—another "This can't be done—but it happened!" The implication in the press was that the House spontaneously reversed its decision as a result of Judge Kelly's comments to the press. The truth is that the first vote by the House was merely a way for those who were trying to impeach Kelly to know who they had to work on to get the measure passed.

Senator Covington was notified about five o'clock on the morning of June 5 that enough votes had been switched for the resolution to pass. This notification shows that it was not the news article that caused the reversal in the House. The accredited source of this item, the newspaper, had not even been delivered at the time Senator Covington was notified of the switch. Rather, it is a clear indication that pressure was applied to some members of the House by some outside source. The fact that Speaker Horne, who had figured so strongly in the proceedings up to this point, and Representative Liles, who was formerly associated with Pasco County, both voted against impeachment on June 4 only to reverse their votes on June 5 clearly indicated dirty politics at work.

Why should the Speaker of the House become so involved in such a case?

Why should it be someone who had formerly been associated with Pasco County to introduce the measure to reconsider when there were 124 representatives present at the time?

Why should such an important matter be voted on with less than seven minutes of discussion?

It is mind-boggling to think that the establishment had the power to change the complete Florida House of Representatives. But the records do show that some fourteen members who voted *No* on the previous day had changed their vote to *Yes*. It is too farfetched to dream that all fourteen spontaneously changed their minds as a result of a newspaper article just off the press and few having been delivered. The speaker had worked all night to change enough votes to go to trial. What was his price? Liles changed his vote in exchange for a judgeship on an appeals court.

The unfairness of the reversal is well summarized in the *Journal of the House of Representatives*, June 4, 1963, p.2629 and June 5, 1963, p.2637:

EXPLANATION OF VOTE ON HOUSE RESOLUTION NO 2504

The situation in Pasco County has been controlled by a few people and they still want control. I respect these people. It was their way of life, but their way is over." These words were allegedly stated by Circuit Judge Richard Kelly to staff writer Tom O'Conner of the *Tampa Tribune* on June 4, 1963, after the House of Representatives had failed to impeach Judge Kelly when it voted on that matter. These words were probably the most unfortunate ones that Judge Kelly ever uttered, if, in fact, he did utter them, but I fail to comprehend how they bear on the question as to whether there was probable cause that Judge Kelly committed specific acts for which he should be removed from office. Further, although an impeachment proceeding in the House of Representatives is more analogous to a Grand Jury proceeding than to a trial, to my way of thinking the Anglo-American concept that no man shall twice be placed in jeopardy for the same offence was overlooked when the House voted to impeach Judge Kelly on June 5, 1963, after it had failed to impeach him in a vote taken the day before. I voted "No" on June 4 because I resolved my serious doubts in favor of the accused. I voted "No" on June 5 because nothing new was introduced to remove these doubts.

Lee Weissenborn
Representative from Dade County

A member of the establishment and member of one of the ruling families was State Senator DeCarr Covington. After the articles of impeachment passed the House, the trial before the senate was set. Senator Covington was approached by members of the establishment to help with a conviction in the senate. He wanted to know the charges. When he decided that this was still a purely political vendetta to get Kelly out of the county so business as usual could return, he refused to participate. Covington's position was that if Kelly were guilty, give him the evidence; if innocent, get off his back. This senator became a very good friend and supporter.

Support for Kelly was growing. Perry Nichols of Miami, considered by many as the Perry Mason of the south, had been reading about the impeachment in the newspapers and became interested. We did not know him before he called and asked Kelly to come to Miami and stay with him for as long as it took him to determine if he wanted to take the case. After more than a week, Mr. Nichols was convinced that Kelly was being railroaded out of office and agreed to take the case pro bono.

Briefly enumerated, the articles of impeachment handed to the senate by the House of Representatives were that Judge Kelly violated the Judicial Code of Ethics as follows (from *Journal of the House of Representatives*, June 5, 1963, pages 2634–2637, inclusive):

Article 1

(a) Judge Kelly charged Clawson, Larkin, and Luckie with contempt and dictated his opinion before the hearing.
(b) He ordered Luckie to appear at a meeting in his office.

(c) He made oppressive statements to Stanley Burnside, clerk of the circuit court.

Article 11

(a) He made a partisan speech at the Zephyrhills Republican Club.

Article 111

(a) He reinstated a temporary injunction in the case of Mountain v. Pinellas County without notice to counsel.

Article 1V

(a) He caused friction between judges over assignment of cases.

Article V

(a) He held that signatures appearing on a pleading at a later date were on pleadings at an earlier date in the case of Hayward v. Hayward. (It is common practice for judges to allow lawyers who inadvertently omit to sign pleadings to do so after filing.

Judge Kelly simply refused to attribute an act of forgery to Mrs. Hayward or her counsel as charged by Mr. Hayward.)

(b) He fined lawyer Alex D. Finch $200 for contempt and later offered to remove same charge and destroy the record.

Article V1

(a) He granted a writ of habeas corpus in State v. Sinclair without notifying prosecuting attorney.

Article V11

(a) He injected his own personality into trials and embarrassed lawyers.
(b) He indulged in partisan politics.
(c) He discussed litigation with parties not in the presence of their attorneys.
(d) He caused confusion by alienating the attorneys.
(e) He flagrantly violated provisions of the Code of Ethics.

(f)   He did commit other acts of misconduct and misdemeanors in office.

Article V111

This article calls for the impeachment trial, the appointment of managers to act in the Senate, and the provision of funds for the same.

The points of law in the articles were resolved to be legal. All other charges indicated the true smallness of the case the House had built.

On June 5, Stanley Burnside, acting as clerk of the circuit court, notified his employees that Judge Kelly could no longer check out materials from his office. This decision was upheld by Circuit Judge B. J. Driver and proved a hardship in the preparation of Kelly's defense.

The senate set September 9, 1963, as the date to begin the impeachment trial. Kelly asked for a two-week delay needed for Perry Nichols of Nichols, Gaither, Beckham, Colson & Spence in Miami—a Democrat, to prepare the case. This was denied, but Mr. Nichols took the case anyway, bringing with him three other lawyers to defend Kelly. Two were from Kelly's home area, Harvey Delzer and B. J. Masterson. Out of the four lawyers, three were registered Democrats.

At the beginning of the trial, Kelly asked that all charges be dismissed. The vote was fifteen to dismiss and twenty-nine opposed. Senator Covington voted for dismissal. The senate then voted separately on each of the articles of impeachment. Two articles were dismissed, and no other article received the two-thirds majority which would be necessary to return a guilty verdict at the end of the trial. The trial continued because the necessary two-thirds majority needed to dismiss the charges was not received.

There was a pronounced display of lack of interest on the part of many of the senators during the trial. Justice Drew had to reprimand the senators several times for lack of attention. Many read newspapers. One could only conclude that many senators felt that the charges were trivial and had made up their minds before the start of the trial, as had so many people throughout the state.

The trial lasted twelve days with forty-five prosecution witnesses being called. All of these witnesses were connected with the law profession in some way. Of the 411,450 people living in the Sixth Judicial Circuit, not one member of the general public testified against Kelly. Even inmates sentenced by Kelly were interviewed by the prosecution. The response was that if tried again, they would want Judge Kelly because he was fair.

After the prosecution had finished calling their witnesses, Representatives O'Neil and Jones, who were acting as house managers, both admitted that they had failed to present one single case for which Kelly should be found guilty but that many small items reached a high total.

At the conclusion of the case presented by the House, Mr. Nichols addressed the senate. He said, "This judge makes mistakes. All judges make mistakes. We are not saying that he does not. We are telling you that the mistakes that have been made are honest mistakes of the heart." This is recorded in the *Journal of the Senate*. Mr. Nichols also marked a quarter of an inch on a yardstick to show that even if all the charges against this judge were true, this would measure his guilt. This yardstick was later framed.

On Tuesday, September 24, 1963, the trial ended; the managers for the House had finished with their presentation of the evidence in support of the articles of impeachment. The attorneys for Judge Kelly presented the court with a motion to dismiss:

1. The evidence and testimony adduced by the State in support of the articles fail to establish beyond and to the exclusion of a reasonable doubt an impeachable offense committed by the respondent.

2. The evidence and testimony adduced by the State is insufficient as a matter of law to establish the validity of the articles of impeachment.

3. The articles of impeachment are insufficient on their face.

4. The evidence and testimony adduced by the State does not establish that the

respondent was guilty of any misdemeanor in office, or any act or omission, involving moral turpitude.

5. The State has utterly failed to produce evidence concerning certain charges in the articles of impeachment.

6. The evidence and testimony introduced by the State does not establish anything more than honest mistakes or errors of law which are reviewable by the appellate courts of the State of Florida.

7. Each individual article merely constitutes criticism of acts taken by the respondent while lawfully operating within the scope of the power vested in him by law, such criticism being of the type that could as well be made of the conduct of any trial judge in the State of Florida.

Senator Ed Price moved that the motion to dismiss the charges against Judge Kelly be granted. The motion was voted upon and carried by twenty-three to twenty. Senator Covington again voted in favor of Judge Kelly.

The presiding officer entered a judgment of acquittal:

> ORDERED AND ADJUDGED, that the Motion to Dismiss be and is hereby granted and the said Richard Kelly be and is hereby acquitted of the charges of said Articles made in said Court.

> DONE AND ORDERED in open Court this twenty-fourth day of September, 1963.

A review of the voting record of the senate shows much more orderliness than a comparable study of the House. Only one senator who voted to impeach Judge Kelly had changed his mind from his original vote to dismiss the charges at the beginning of the trial. This was Senator Usher of Chiefland. Therefore, after all its witnesses had been heard, the prosecution had only won one juror and had lost ten for a net loss of nine votes. Surely, had the trial gone to completion, Judge Kelly would have been cleared by an even larger margin.

Perry Nichols, Manager Jones and Judge Kelly

It is interesting to note that Kelly's lawyers had subpoenaed at least one juror from every case that he had presided over. Surely he had to be certain of his own innocence in order to take such a risk, for unfavorable testimony from a juror would have meant serious trouble.

The trial cost the taxpayers over $125,000 with $29,995 going to the house managers Daniel, Jones, and O'Neil. Some 2,657 pages of transcript in the *Journal of the Senate* records this personal grudge so that historians might laugh at this absurd attempt at revenge on the part of this Pasco judge.

In a later interview with Judge Kelly, it was reported that he felt the moves against him were partisan rather than personal. The clique did not fear Kelly because he was a Republican; rather, the clique feared him only to the degree that he placed the clique in danger and would forever change their way of life. It was partisan in that it involved the clique and the anti-clique. It was personal in that the two sides were respectively insiders and outsiders. This is an important concept.

Some of the lawyers never got over the fact that the young upstart lawyer from Zephyrhills defeated longtime circuit judge Orville Dayton, a fixture in Pasco County politics. The lawyers around Dade City had grown accustomed to Dayton and to having their way around the courthouse. It was written that "Kelly's defeating this veteran Democratic judge coupled with his clean-up of the county while a U.S. prosecutor brought the wrath of the 'establishment' in Pasco County down upon him."

As a circuit judge, Kelly changed the way of doing business of the court. He did not like it when a defendant had been in jail too long without his day in court. He stopped the practice of automatically sending fathers who failed to pay their child support into the orange groves owned by a prominent attorney to work off their debts. And he would bend over backward to see that a poor defendant facing serious criminal charges got his day in court.

But regardless of the fact that the clique used their immense power to endanger his whole way of life, Judge Kelly expressed sympathy for them because he felt the members of the clique knew no other way of life.

It was also reported that Judge Kelly did not look upon himself as a leader and felt that a change would eventually have taken place without him. He did not take credit for awakening the politically sleeping people of the county. But in effect, he was a leader. It was the image which he created that spurred the people. Here was a man who dared to oppose the clique with full knowledge of the possible consequences, fought them on their own grounds, and defeated them. Never before in the history of Pasco County had anyone dared to oppose the clique, much less win even a small victory. This win was the beginning of a hope in the future and renewed pride in government.

We left Tallahassee to return home to our two small children, Sherri and John, who were ages two and three at the time. They were being cared for by friends and neighbors. At one point during the trial, their lives were threatened. The children were in hiding for their safety at a friend's home in

Ocala until the trial was over. Our bank accounts and records had been closed to us. Knowing that anything could happen, we had taken money out of the bank and had hidden it in the hems of the draperies in our bedroom.

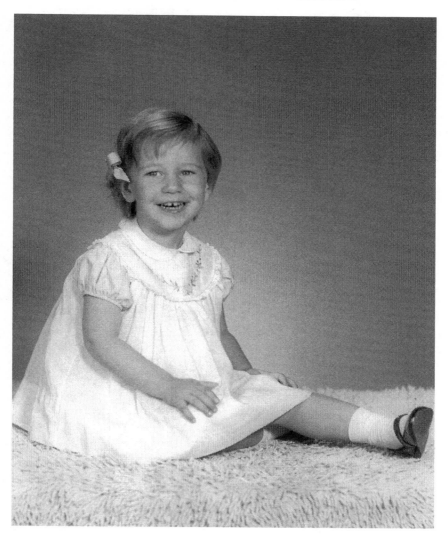

The beginning of the impeachment trial was on September 9, 1963. Perry Nichols, Kelly's lawyer for the impeachment trial, had delivered the commencement address at Stetson College of Law in St. Petersburg, Florida, on June 12 before Kelly's trial. The title of his speech was "The Curse of Conformity and a Recipe for Happiness," and he gave a copy to Kelly. After reading the speech, I understood why he wanted to defend Kelly.

Nichols spoke to the young lawyers graduating from Stetson, telling them the most common obstruction encountered on the path to success is what he chose to call "the curse of conformity."

> As a lawyer you will be given the opportunity to develop your entire personality and to express yourself as an *individual. Individuality*, as distinguished from *conformity*, has become a rare quality. It has become increasingly difficult to resist the multifarious daily pressures of conformity.
>
> Throughout your entire life, those all around you will constantly be suggesting—directly

and indirectly—that you strive for security. The clichés of conformity, "Don't rock the boat," "Be popular," "Be a nice guy," "Play it safe," "Why take a chance?" have unfortunately gained unwarranted prominence in our society.

Conformists do not vary their approach to any facet of their daily lives. Their behavior is characterized by an almost ludicrous and unbending rigidity.

To be a successful lawyer, or to be a successful businessman, one must be a "rugged individualist" who *can* and *will* think and act independently. The conformist is not born. He is made, influenced by the people around him.

Heaven help the man who dares to be different in thought or action. Any deviation from the mediocre norm, will brand you. He will be tagged immediately by his conformist friends as a "controversial person," the worst tag that can be affixed to anyone in a conformist society.

This, of course, is sheer nonsense. Any man who allows his individuality to assert itself *constructively* will soon rise to the top.

As a successful attorney, there will be times in your life when you will have to stand up and be counted, and the stand may not always be a popular one.

These are excerpts from Perry Nichols's speech to young lawyers. The entire speech should be printed here. I think he saw a rare quality in Kelly; Kelly walked the talk.

The second part of the speech was just as important. Success without happiness is empty. When you blend success and happiness together, you have all that one can hope for or ever hope to achieve.

"An Evening of Honors" at the Opera honoring the
Sebrings as guests of Anthony "Tony" Battaglia
(December 4, 1965). From left to right: Judge
Richard Kelly, Mrs. Sebring, Loraine Kelly, and
Dean Sebring of the Stetson Law School

7

A LULL BEFORE MORE TRIALS TO COME

Lean on Thee; grow in grace

Attitudes changed and support grew for Kelly and for me. I was asked to join a chapter of the Zephyrhills Garden Club. All clubs outside political ones had been closed to me before the trials. This was significant since the president of the local garden club was a state democratic committee member. I thanked them sincerely, but I felt that I could not and should not join at that time. They insisted with the promise that I would not be put to work until I was ready. Even so, at the first meeting attended, I was given a program to choose an entry for the next flower show.

Not knowing enough to make a choice to enter the flower show, I gave the program to Sherri and let her choose for me. She was about six at that time. A judge was looking at my entry before it was judged and told me that I could not do what

I had done. It was my interpretation of "The Good Earth," and I had to go with it; it was too late to change. When the judging was over, Sherri and I had won first prize. We went on to win a prize for every other entry.

In February 1971, "Mrs. Kelly is Elected New President of Garden Club."

Most treasured was a note from Anne Gall, one of the insiders and a Democrat, who wrote, "Congratulations for a job well done. I *know* a lot of planning and thought went into your job, and it showed. The town is a happier place because of all the effort you put forth."

One could have thought that with all the trials going on, nothing else could be accomplished. Even so, Kelly served as a member of the Florida Bar Association's Committee on Judicial Administration and was a leader in procedural and judicial reform in the circuit court. He introduced the two-stage trial in capital cases, the bifurcated trial, which became an accomplished reform in the procedures of Florida criminal law. He had long advocated improvements in court administration and court reform which were adopted.

In 1966, Kelly ran for reelection to the circuit court and won easily. This was another disappointing loss for the clique.

The *Zephyrhills News*, November 10, 1966, reported:

> Judge Richard Kelly of Zephyrhills, who was elected to his first six-year term by a squeak-through margin in 1960, won 69 percent of Pasco County's votes this time.

The establishment does not give up easily. The impeachment effort had failed, and their mission to get rid of this judge not yet accomplished. Therefore, at the first opportunity, an amendment appeared on the ballot, introduced by Representative Tommy Stevens, nephew of the clerk of the circuit court, creating a Judicial Qualifications Commission. And who do you think was the first judge to come before the handpicked commission? You guessed it: Richard Kelly.

The law stated that the accused judge's case would be heard in his own courtroom behind closed doors. The judge then could be found guilty, and the public could be told that they did not hear the case, therefore, must accept the ruling of the commission. January 21, 1969, Kelly filed a demand before the state supreme court under the Sunshine rule. The demand automatically released all information filed in the case and compelled the commission to open the hearing to the public. The commission had begun an unpublicized investigation of Kelly in June 1968. As soon as the doors were opened and the public was allowed to witness the trial, again the establishment failed *even though* in the middle of the trial when it was evident that they were losing the case, Kelly was charged with insanity—another "This can't be done—but it happened!" This was a shocker and contrary to the rules. Every person, by law, has a right to know before trial for what he is being accused. He was not only charged with insanity, but he was to appear before psychiatrists chosen by the commission. Of course the psychiatrists would be instructed to find Kelly unfit. Kelly was most willing to be examined. Understandably, he would rather be examined by clinics chosen by his family doctor, Dr. Harry Brownlee. Dr.

Brownlee arranged appointments with Duke University and Johns Hopkins. Kelly was not only found to be sane, but declared, in their opinion, most suited for the position he held. A doctor from Johns Hopkins was so incensed by what was happening that he flew down to Dade City at his own expense to testify for Kelly. However, as soon as he was called and took the stand, he was dismissed after identifying himself and was not allowed to speak. Kelly often quipped that he was the only judge, and later congressman, certified sane.

An Editorial Viewpoint in *the Zephyrhills News*, May 15, 1969, stated:

Abolish the Commission

Richard Kelly is stronger now than at any time in his career. Word of his reprimand has been greeted not with nods of agreement but with resentment directed at the Judicial Qualifications Commission. An image of Judge Kelly as a "People's Judge" has been firmly implanted in the minds of most voters in his circuit.

Senator DeCarr Covington was asked to be the featured speaker at a public rally given at the New Port Richey Recreation Center sponsored by "Citizens for Judge Kelly." His message was important because he was a birthright member of the clique who found a conscience and was brave enough to stand for what was right and just, no matter the consequences.

> Speech by D. D. Covington, Jr., given at the New Port Richey Recreation Center, New Port Richey, Florida, on March 1, 1969
>
> D. D. Covington: Can you hear me in the back? Glenn, I would like to thank you for the fine introduction. You know, it has been over two years since I have had an opportunity to speak to anyone other than my wife at home. She doesn't always speak as kindly to me as you have, so I really appreciate it.
>
> John Brasher and Reverend McCart, Mrs. Lindsay, Pat Hodges, Ron Fischer, Commander, Dolly Posey, Reverend Bretcher, Bob, members of the press, fellow Confederates, and friends of Judge Kelly:

I am here tonight to talk about an old and dear and good friend of mine and relate to you a little of the history, past, present and future, which makes the two of us long, fast, and firm friends.

Several years ago, when I was newly elected to the Florida state senate, I announced to the press that I was introducing a bill with the intention of changing Pasco County and the part they play in the Sixth Judicial Circuit and move this to the county to the north, the neighboring county to the north. I had some very good reasons, and I stated them to the press. We had more in common with the people to the north, and, after all, those people are neighbors up there and so forth and so on, but as the truth will out and as those of you who have been on the scene a long time know, at that time, I was a member of what is known as "The Establishment," and I was acting on behalf of "The Establishment," and we had one purpose, and that purpose was to remove the then circuit judge from Pasco County as the law would require and send him back to Pinellas County where all those bad Republicans were.

Pretty soon I began to hear some rumors. These rumors were that there were some petitions being circulated. Of course, I couldn't imagine why there would be any petitions being circulated about anything I did because I was a member of "The Establishment" and anything "The Establishment" did in Pasco County had to be right. So I ignored these rumors and went straight ahead. And I had an opportunity to meet this Republican judge and discuss this matter with him on two or three different occasions.

The talks were very pleasant. He always left with me saying, "Judge, people in Pinellas County like you. You will enjoy it over there."

Soon, some of the people I live with every day, not political people but people who I have a lot of confidence in, said, "DeCarr, you are doing a bad thing and a wrong thing." They said, "You are going to have to get straightened out about this." I said,

"Oh, no, I am an elected senator, and I am not concerned about this. Whatever I do will be fine with the people." Then those petitions began to get a lot of names on them. Something began to happen to me. My political conscience began to be aroused.

I tried to gather all those people together who wanted the judicial change, get them all in the same room, and I said to them, "Now, fellows, I've been out front." Two or three wanted me to get out front. I said, "I am trying to do what you wanted me to do, but I am in trouble. I need some people to help me." They said, "Old buddy, go out there and get this taken care of." I said, "Fellows, I begin to feel something in the air, and I believe there is going to be trouble down the line. I need some people to help." They said, "No, you are not going to have any trouble." I said, "Fellows, I don't want to go out of this room if we don't have an understanding about what we are going to do. Help me out of the problem we are going to have. If we don't have a public referendum on this bill and let the people decide this, then I am not going to introduce the bill." They said, "No, don't worry about that. We will talk to you about that tomorrow." All the fellows scattered out in various directions, and I sent them all telegrams. I said, "Fellows, I asked you to help me, and you won't help me, and you don't want the people to vote on this change, and I am not going to introduce this bill."

This doesn't mean that all of a sudden I was a hero. I was just another politician getting out of trouble.

So I weathered that storm. I still didn't know this man. I just met him once or twice. Then this very select core of "The Establishment" called me in and said, "Now, since we can't change the circuit, we are going to impeach this Republican judge." I said, "Fellows, I don't care if you hang him. I am not having anything to do with it. I have already gotten the message."

Sure enough they got busy and took this thing to Tallahassee and spent not only

$125,000 of the taxpayer's money but in excess of $190,000 of the taxpayer's money. And they began to get on this judge sort of serious.

We have a lot of good people in politics, better than I was at the time, and the House heard all these charges, and they said there wasn't anything to it. They dismissed it, and incidentally, in between the time they said that and this happened, I again sat in a room, but I was a little worried about the people in "The Establishment" now, because things—it didn't look like these fellows were really my friends, so I took along some friends of mine, and we had another meeting. There were some different people there, but Judge Kelly was there, and an offer was made to Judge Kelly at that time which came; and I can't specifically identify him, but I am sure it did come from the floor manager for impeachment in the House, that if he would take a reprimand they would let him go scot-free. Now, we went around that room, thirteen of us in there, and all of us expressed an opinion.

Some of his friends begged him to take the deal. I know that when it came to me I said that he was either guilty or innocent.

I know that Senator Young was there and said, "Judge, you have got an obligation to follow through on this thing." And I know that Judge Kelly had his turn. He said, "Fellows, there just isn't any question about it. I owe it to the people to follow through and not to make a deal." So we went on to where the House said he wasn't guilty, and at six o'clock the next morning, lo and behold, "The Establishment" was at my house.

I had rented a house in Tallahassee. They said, "Now, DeCarr, we are in bad trouble." The House turned him loose. We have been working all night, been up all night and haven't had one minute's sleep. We have been out working on this thing, trying to get the House to change its vote, but we didn't make it. They are not going to reconsider. They said, "We have got to have the circuit change badly. And they stayed at my house from six o'clock—until they got a phone call, until, I believe, a quarter to nine, nine o'clock. The House had gone in session and reconsidered and voted out the articles of impeachment against Judge Kelly.

I will tell you, right along about there is when I stopped being a politician and began to realize there was something basically wrong with what was going on.

Now, the next day or that same day, even though these articles were voted out, that same circuit change bill came rotating down to the senate, and they had a man standing right there with me. And I had to get up right in front of everybody and say no, and the local bill got killed. We didn't change the circuit. The senate adjourned. The House adjourned, and we went home after the normal course of business.

In the intervening months—and if you think you are familiar with pressure tactics and behind-the-scene maneuvering and things that are just plain down-right dishonest— as a member of the senate I was pledged not to discuss this case with anyone. I can't think of the dozens of people that were sent to me in private and in public, quietly and vociferously and in belligerent and kindly manner to influence me without ever hearing the evidence to convict this Republican judge. My answer at that time and throughout this trial was that we weren't supposed to discuss it. And, as a matter of fact, anyone caught discussing it was subject to contempt of the senate; if I discussed it, I was subject to be reprimanded or even dismissed from the senate.

We went back to Tallahassee, and we heard this case. I saw the maneuvering in the lounge, the men's room and not the floor manager but the prosecutor and the floor managers in the senate who had old cronies and old buddies who had gone to them, and I saw people who I had had a lot of respect for and thought were great, fine senators become small men in my eyes because of their actions behind the scene.

We heard that case, and I got to know a lot about this man in hearing the case.

Here we were spending the taxpayers' money, and we had people who had investigated every aspect of his life. They were looking for something bad about him. You know, he is human. Why they didn't find something bad, because he is human and surely he had something bad someplace, but they didn't find one thing to bring before that senate that warranted even someone raising their voice. And before the senate ever heard one word of defense on Judge Kelly's behalf, we moved that the charges be dismissed and immediately moved that the senate adjourn sine die and start brand new. And this man who had been so put upon and whose family had suffered so much and whose life had been opened to the sunshine of public opinion so much was returned to his rightful place on the bench of the Sixth Judicial Circuit of the State of Florida.

Now, I still didn't know this man well. But this man had had a tremendous, vibrant, violent effect on my life. And I am certain that whatever conscience in the public life—whatever actions I took from that time on as a public servant—that I was in a large part influenced by the kind of person this man was, by the example he set and by having to take a stand which might have been just a little unpopular here, a little unpopular there, controversial and not smart politics there. And, you know, I was just amazed. I think that was the beginning of the time the people displayed some confidence in me. I think it was my good fortune, from that date on, to enjoy the confidence of the people who sent me to the senate and not only in public life but [also] in private life. A large part of that I owe to this Republican judge.

In the years following, Judge Kelly and I did get to know each other. I got to know that this man came from a very poor origin. I know he had to struggle all through his boyhood. I know he joined the Marines and was a combat veteran of four years before he ever graduated from high school. He came back and completed his education and worked his way through college and for a while was a school teacher. He came back to Florida and went to law school. He practiced law right here in Pasco County before going with the federal government where he was one of the more successful federal prosecutors. I learned all this about a man that I had been willing, with introduction of this bill, to take away his right to serve the people or part of the people that elected him.

We got to playing a little tennis together. He was a pretty good tennis player. He played on his college team. I had never played tennis. We discussed philosophy, religion, basic human relations. We have spent literally hundreds and hundreds and hundreds of hours together. I think we both have real concern for many of the things that were happening, not only in Pasco County and this judicial circuit, but [also] in the State of Florida and in our country and all over the world. We talked about those things as friends will, and the more we talked the more we argued, and the more we ran up against each other the faster and firmer friends we became.

I met his wife and children. I was in his home many times. They were in our home, and I think maybe from the mutual adversity we suffered in Tallahassee—because I suffered along with him, one way or another—and through, maybe, the better times, and maybe through the heat and fire of good and bad times we became tremendous friends. I probably know this man better than anyone in Pasco County or Pinellas County and with one or two exceptions better than anyone in the State of Florida except his own family. And he is a good man and a fine friend.

And that brings me to my purpose for being here. I know his little girl, Sherri, and I would hope for her that she might have the patience and fortitude and charm of her mother. I would hope for his son, John, that he might stand tall among men like his father does. I would hope for his wife, Loraine, the good Lord would give her strength to proceed on and put this nightmare behind her family. For my friend the judge, I would certainly hope that he would have the wisdom of Solomon, the patience of Job, long life and good times and comfort in his chosen profession, the law, and above all justice.

DeCarr gave us the original copy of his speech to use as we wished. He would have been pleased that it has been included in our story. He and Kelly remained good friends and stayed in touch as long as they lived.

Political power has long arms. Kelly was weathering the storms. But how much can a man endure and survive? Kelly, a maverick, was willing to go where others would not; this courage and persistence spoke volumes about him.

8

A JUDGE SEES PRISON . . .

Gained experience in order to sentence justly

The summer of 1970, the children and I went with Kelly to attend the National College of State Trial Judges held on the campus of the University of Nevada in Reno. This was good for us to be together and to enjoy time out from fighting political battles.

We and the other judges' families lived in dorms, and we even took some classes. Sherri took Spanish and later minored in Spanish at Vanderbilt University. The judges were busy during the day, but during most evenings and weekends, we enjoyed Reno and all it had to offer. We went to shows, did sightseeing, took side trips—even San Francisco—and enjoyed outings with the other families. This was big for us.

During the conference, it was suggested to the judges that it would be helpful in their sentencing if they submitted themselves to a prison so that they could know personally what they were imposing with the sentences they gave. Out of this large group of judges, I never heard how many of the other judges completed this assignment while in Nevada or later. I did hear many say, "No way." This was another act of bravery and courage for Kelly—he did both, in Nevada and Florida.

After this experience, Kelly wrote an article that appeared on the front page of the *St. Petersburg Times*, January 19, 1971. A copy of the article follows. By his own words, one can better know the man.

A JUDGE SEES PRISON, FROM THE INSIDE
By Judge Richard Kelly Sixth
Judicial Circuit, Florida

Florida's prison system (the Division of Corrections) is in serious trouble.

The problems are varied and difficult, and include:

Grossly inadequate care of the mentally ill. Those with deep-seeded mental troubles are mingled in the general prison population to their own detriment and the rest of the prisoners.

Failure of those on the executive and legislative level to provide the leadership necessary to give direction to the whole penal process.

Serious racial tension, which is demonstrated by de facto segregation the prisoners impose on themselves.

Meaningful rehabilitation is not attainable in the atmosphere that exists due to understaffing, overcrowding, lack of sufficient programs aimed at improving the attitude of prisoners, a belief among the prisoners that corruption exists among the guards in the form of pilfering and smuggling, and the fact the parole commission functions in a way that is insensitive and arbitrary (a view shared by prison authorities as well as the inmates).

To enter a prison to see it is one thing; to go there to appreciate and understand it is something else.

What it represents and its sadness are overwhelming. The raw ends of all human futility are exposed in this place.

Thousands of men are jammed together with fear and hopelessness—fear of each other, of themselves, and the future.

Raiford's East Unit is the maximum security prison where 1,150 of the most troubled prisoners are housed. From looking at the faces and listening to the sounds, it seemed that it would be more natural for everyone to sit down and cry in despair. Instead, there was laughter that was out of tune, bravado, and hostility. Most surprising, there was hope, instinctive and unsure.

These are the prisoners who wait on death row and await the end of long sentences in solitary cells. These are the worst—the ones society feared most and the rest of the prison system had rejected as incorrigible and treacherous.

The presence of death row permeated the whole place. I talked at length with two inmates whose death sentences had been commuted to life. We talked of their waiting and the prison. Many on death row have been there for years, one more than ten.

The really shocking situation is the number of inmates with deep-seated mental problems trying to survive in a situation that would be tough for a man with a strong mind.

I saw a boy, small in stature, standing in a cage, dressed in white coveralls. The front of his clothes and hands were covered with blood, and he was crying like a baby. He had just mutilated his sex organ. I tried to talk to him. He didn't know I was in the same world.

I talked to another prisoner who had just recently slashed himself and severed his Achilles tendon. He was in special confinement awaiting his release. His term was up, and he was on his way to being free to go among the public.

I talked with another inmate who believed he was "the Christ" and was in league with "Nixon." He was confused when I told him I was a judge. I felt sick to my stomach to think he was in these surroundings in the name of decent people.

I talked to a boy in his teens who wanted permission to call his wife, who was divorcing him. He was in the hospital—he had mutilated himself.

It is rare to talk to any prisoner who doesn't admit to a mental or emotional problem. They don't see how they could do the things they did if they didn't have a problem.

The facilities for treating the mentally ill are, for practical purposes, non-existent. The system must depend upon the state mental hospital. The state hospital has more problems than it can handle and too little money and staff to be willing to take on the problems of the prison. Whatever the reason, the deplorable conditions exist.

The main hospital for the whole prison system is at Raiford. This hospital is poorly maintained; proper sanitation is wanting. There were empty rooms, and at the same time, there were beds in the halls. Prisoners were manning sensitive positions such as general hospital supply.

The quality of food in the Reception and Medical Center, the East Unit, and Main Unit at Raiford was good for prison fare but not well prepared. The breads baked in the prison were good. The "clean" dishes at the Main Unit were extremely greasy. The food was the same at Sumter Correctional Institute but much better prepared and more palatable.

There is a system of prison canteens in which prisoners can buy a wide variety of wares including foods such as ice cream and even filets and chops in some cases. A huge percentage of the prisoners are without the funds to share in this. This whole canteen affair could stand an examination.

On the morning shift of Dec. 22, there were 26 guards for the East Unit. Four went to the towers and 22 went "inside" to guard, watch, and supervise 1,150 inmates.

This understaffing leads to a multitude of ills including homosexuality in all its forms; perverted prostitution and rape, the latter usually blacks attacking whites.

When the staff is engaged beyond its capacity in this fashion there just isn't time for sufficient staff training and supervision. This results in the prisoners' complaint that the prison rules change with every guard, which deteriorates morale and creates hostility.

The overcrowding of the inmates at the Main Unit and the Receiving Center is severe and sure to get worse. At the center, cells designed for one man house three, and the institution is only two years old.

The guards are fed at the prison, for which they are to pay 35¢ per meal. The food is supposed to be the same as that eaten by the prisoners but fed in staff mess halls. The prisoners doubt it, and one said he has seen the guards avoid paying.

I saw rolls nearly burned in the prisoner mess and golden brown in the staff mess. This is a bad practice. There should be a privately owned restaurant unconnected with the prison for the guards, or the guards should bring their lunches. This is the practice in the Nevada penal system, and it works better.

There is widespread belief among the prisoners that the guards pilfer everything that is loose, including bicycles being refurbished by prisoners for poor children.

This is all a problem even if untrue. I am convinced the prisoners believe that this corruption exists, plus believing that one can buy "anything" while in prison if he has the money, and they believe that guards participate in this smuggling.

It is a certainty, however, that the vast majority of the guards do an outstanding job under the circumstances, or the whole thing wouldn't hold together, but this doesn't alter the situation.

If our prisons were austere, hard, clean, and fair and free of corruption, we could house the inmates decently and do it within the present budget. The prisoners would respect us, and we could respect each other. This would constitute honest punishment without excuse. In this atmosphere much rehabilitation would take place.

As it is, the whole system has lost its credibility. The inmates see through the fraud of the talked-about rehabilitation and vocational training, recognizing that one can't take place in such an atmosphere and that the other is just talk. They have contempt for a society that sends its children and insane to live with felons in a situation none in the free world would believe.

Because we, as a people, or the responsible leaders on the executive and legislative level, lack the courage to make a decision, we vacillate between the punishment and the rehabilitative theories and lose what we could obtain by trying to accomplish the frills without making the necessary commitments.

Until there is an enlightened decision to really help the prisoners, to supply the people and money to get the job done, the emphasis should be on cleanliness, decency, and integrity. Vocational training and education and the like must be considered secondary. These programs aren't going to have the full measure of help if the inmate considers society itself unjust and corrupt.

The prisons are an important part of the law enforcement cycle. If the attitude of the felon sent there isn't changed toward respecting the law and the principles of honesty, we haven't seen the peak of the rise in crime.

The light of hope is the administrative personnel in the system. Without exception these men are capable and enthusiastic.

They believe in what can be done. They consider the prisoners as human beings and believe them salvageable. If these people had the funds and support, Florida's prisons would serve us well.

JUDGE KELLY'S LOGBOOK ON HIS DAYS AS INMATE

Statement from Judge Richard Kelly:

In July 1970, I spent parts of two days and one night in the medium security unit of the Nevada State Penitentiary at Carson City, Nevada.

I was transported by prison bus from Reno to the maximum security unit of the prison on July 8 and actually went through the induction process. Dressed entirely in prison clothes, including underwear, I was transported to the medium security unit. On arrival I was assigned a bed. I walked through the prison gates without a guard or any prison personnel and met a prisoner who was sent to show me my assigned bed.

From the time I entered the gate I mingled with the prisoners and had no escort or contact with guards except routine encounters, which were few until I left the next day.

I slept in a dorm-type room where 10 prisoners slept. Their crimes included murder, robbery, rape, and arson. I had complete freedom of the whole unit, all buildings, the same as prisoners. I ate in the mess halls at the same tables under the same conditions as any inmate.

On December 20, I started a tour of the Reception and Medical Center at Lake Butler, Florida, the main and east units of the state prison at Raiford and the Sumter Correctional Institution at Bushnell. This included two nights and three days.

I spent a night and half a day at the reception center, a half day and one night in the Raiford East Unit, one day in the Main Unit, and one day at Sumter.

While in the Raiford East Unit, I toured the facility with a supervisor. I had the opportunity to talk with the prisoners privately at my choosing during the tour. I ate punishment rations ("dog food" or soup) and tap water for my night meal.

During the evening I talked with prisoners unattended by prison personnel until 11 p.m. I then was locked in a "segregated confinement" cell without a mattress until 1 a.m. and then transported to a regular individual cell with a standard prison mattress for the rest of the night. I was up and about the unit again at 6 a.m.

The visits in the other units combined guarded tours and individual investigations as I wished.

At the Raiford main unit and at Sumter I entered the chow line unescorted and ate at the tables with the prisoners of my choice with only the one regular mess hall guard.

At no time was there interference from the administration or guards. I found the cooperation and candor of the administration and prisoners to be excellent. (Reprinted by permission of the *Tampa Bay Times*, all rights reserved)

Because of Kelly's knowledge of prison conditions and the problems of punishment based on personal prison inspections, years of prosecution while serving as a federal prosecutor and from serving on the bench, Kelly was called to Washington to testify before the Congressional House Select Committee on Organized Crime investigating Florida's prisons.

9

ON TO WASHINGTON

The Little Man Loses a Friend on the Bench

We, the Kelly family, moved to Holiday on the west side of the county in 1970. The west side was the more populated and had never had a resident judge. The east side had always held the power. We found a good church home, and the children were enjoying school and having friends close by. They had moved from the grove to the city with neighbors and sidewalks, and this was fun. We had a very large play area and a pool; therefore, our home quickly became the gathering place for the neighborhood. The children still enjoyed their horses but had to board them. Sherri enjoyed competing in horse shows with friends. John chose to break wild horses. He tamed a few. The family was settling in, and I was in no hurry to make another move.

Kelly was reelected to the circuit court without opposition in 1972.

Public support and Kelly's interest continued to grow in running for Congress to represent the Fifth Congressional District. The district included Pasco, Hernando, Citrus, Sumter, Lake, Seminole, and parts of Orange and Pinellas Counties, making it the largest district in the United States, population-wise.

Kelly sought the counsel of his good friend and law school classmate Tony Battaglia in making this decision. When asked, "What would you think if I told you that I was running for Congress?" Tony recalls saying, "I think you're crazy as hell. You have fourteen years on the bench, and you're in a secure position." Some could say maybe he should have listened.

Battaglia and Kelly met in 1951 as law students at the University of Florida. They spent summers in search of watermelon patches for the New York produce company Battaglia's father owned. All these years later they had remained friends with a lot of miles traveled together.

Kelly resigned in his fourteenth year as circuit judge to become a candidate for Congress to represent the Fifth District. This campaign was to be quite an undertaking.

The *St. Petersburg Times*, April 3, 1974, commented as follows regarding the judge's service on the bench:

> The Little Man Loses a Friend on the Bench
>
> The entry of Circuit Judge Richard Kelly into the 5th Congressional District race removes a controversial—and conscientious—figure from the judicial family.
>
> Kelly made local political history in 1960 when he was elected to the Pasco bench as a Republican in a solidly Democratic county. He unseated a veteran Democratic jurist with close ties to the entrenched East Pasco "establishment" that controlled the county at that time—and the old-timers never forgave him.
>
> Kelly twice survived attempts to remove him from office, in which not only his conduct on the bench—but also his sanity—was

questioned. Throughout his ordeals, he maintained his sense of humor, and he once quipped privately that he was the only judge in the 6th Judicial District who was certified sane.

The ouster efforts and a subsequent reprimand by the Florida Supreme Court did not diminish his popularity with the voters. After his initial election, he was reelected twice.

Although he was disliked by many lawyers—some of whom he publicly reprimanded and even held in contempt—Kelly never lost touch with the "little man," who often appeared before him as a defendant.

He consistently bent over backward to make sure that all defendants, rich or poor, received a fair trial in his court. And the door to his chamber was always open. No one needed an appointment to see him.

Kelly was a tireless worker. He started his day early, and he finished late. He often "brown-bagged" his lunch in his chamber during a recess in a trial, and he sometimes held court at night and on the weekends.

His object was to speed the judicial process and to keep his docket current. In that task, he was highly successful.

Kelly's sometimes unorthodox methods frequently brought him into disfavor with his fellow jurists, but in our view he was a good judge. We are sorry to see him leave the Pasco bench.

Whether he would make a good congressman—if elected—is another matter. We shall reserve our judgment on that score until he makes known his views on the pressing issues with which a congressman must deal. (Reprinted by permission of the *Tampa Bay Times*, all rights reserved)

The *St. Petersburg Times*, August 31, 1974, endorsement:

In going with Kelly we leaned heavily on his record of independence and honesty on the bench . . . He is known as a ruggedly independent, tireless worker . . . We expect that as a congressman he would act on conscience, not as a party loyalist or organization man.

Our grassroots organizational experience gained early on kept serving us well. The National Republican Organization felt that there was no way that a small town judge could possibly run a campaign for Congress without their help. They insisted on sending a Washingtonian as our campaign manager. This was a disaster and was costly. The same procedures and practices used in the earlier campaigns should work well again, even though the boundaries were much bigger. We had the added advantage of my having served two years as district #1 chairman of the Westminster Presbytery serving nine churches in seven cities in the Fifth Congressional District.

1974 was a long year of campaigning, and the children were real troopers. We could not have been successful without the tremendous support of so many who joined us in this undertaking.

The campaign was successful, and we began making our plans for the move to Washington. A big send-off was planned to celebrate. What an opportunity for all of us, both our family and the Fifth Congressional District.

A photo of Kelly on the Capitol steps appeared on the front page of the *Washington Post*.

We went to Washington as a family for the orientation and to find a place to live. I had only seen the Capitol from a train window as I was traveling from Georgia to New York during my youth to visit friends the Klingenbecks. Never in my wildest dreams did I ever think that one day this would be home.

With the help of a good real estate agent and a good map of Washington and the surrounding area, the hunt for a home began. A star marking the Capitol on the map and a circle around Fairfax County with the best schools was my guide in choosing a home with the shortest drive for Kelly to the hill and good schools for the children. The newspapers had much to say about the house we chose in Franklin Park, McLean, Virginia, and my "engineering" the move. Buying any house in Washington was much more expensive than buying one in Pasco County, Florida.

We then returned to Florida to prepare for the transition. The election in early November and the Ninety-fourth Congress convening in early January when Kelly would take the oath of office left little time to close a house and get relocated.

We arrived in McLean a few days before the movers. Our new neighbors were incredibly helpful. Much to the children's delight, a record snowfall welcomed our arrival. Our new home was located on a hill, and with sleds furnished by neighbors, the children enjoyed snow such as they had never seen before. Driving to the Capitol was a challenge; driving anywhere in the snow was a challenge for us.

Kelly was sworn in as a member of the Ninety-fourth Congress on January 3, 1975, with his family in the balcony.

Gerald Ford was president at that time, having just taken office on August 9, 1974, following the resignation of President Richard Nixon over the Watergate scandal. Ford became the first unelected president in the nation's history. He had been appointed vice president less than a year earlier by President Nixon after Spiro Agnew resigned.

The average member of Congress represented about 484,000 people, but the Fifth District of Florida had the distinction of being the largest and fastest-growing congressional district in the nation. With 642,000 residents at that time and more coming in every day, the district presented some unique challenges to the congressman who wanted to serve effectively and keep in touch with the people.

The work for Kelly as a new member of Congress was full time. He was well received in Congress and was prepared for the task. He vigorously sought after appointments to the committees that would increase his effectiveness to serve his constituents. He served on the Committee on Banking, Housing, and Currency and the Committee on Agriculture, as well as subcommittees within these committees. In Banking, the subcommittees were Economic Stabilization, Housing and Community Development, and International Trade, Investment, and Monetary Policy. In Agriculture, the subcommittees were Conservation and Credit, Dairy and Poultry, and Forests. "As a member of these committees, I can help write legislation that will benefit not only our major industries, such as farming and housing, but every taxpayer and consumer in the Fifth District."

Kelly was also dealing with getting his offices in Washington and the District organized to do the best job possible for the people he served. A proper balance of experienced hill staffers and capable, loyal workers from home was necessary. This was not easy to accomplish in such a short period of time. Meetings and speaking engagements would require many trips back to Florida.

The Committee for the Survival of a Free Congress published the results of its study of the voting record of each congressional representative. Kelly was proud to receive one of the highest anti-inflation ratings in Congress. He was off to a good start.

During the first year in Washington, I made almost as many trips back home as Kelly did. My message was that I had been given a front row seat in Washington by them. This was a privilege and a responsibility. Come to Washington; everything available to me would also be available to them.

The Hornbuckles from Dade City were among many who accepted this offer. I had arranged a special White House tour available to congressional wives before the public was allowed in. We were usually received in a reception room and served coffee before seeing this beautiful home in a way not available to the general public on tour. The morning of the tour with the Hornbuckles, I received a call from the White House asking if I would mind finding my own parking place for this time. In exchange, my guests and I were invited to be a part of the welcoming ceremony for the Emperor and Empress of Japan. We were delighted. I was told that President Ford was aware of my invitations to the people of the Fifth District in Florida and was pleased.

I had met the other wives of the new members of the Ninety-fourth Congress and bonded rather quickly considering I was one of the very few Republican wives to go to Washington in 1974. In fact, Kelly was one of only two of the ten freshman Republicans to be elected in that Watergate year and the only one from the south and the border states.

To Loraine Kelly
   Hope your years in Washington are as
   enjoyable as mine have been,

                              Betty Ford

10

THE BEGINNING OF THE DOWNFALL

A personal tragedy

About six months after our move to Washington and with all seemingly going well, I received a phone call from a friend in Orlando who was a volunteer during the campaign telling me that trouble was on its way. After hearing what she had to tell me, I thought that I could better handle the problem in Washington than in Florida. This brought to mind a warning given to me during the campaign by Hazel and Doug, friends and supporters. Little did I know how very big this problem would become and how it would affect our lives.

During that campaign year, Kelly had met a Judith Foley at a Young Republicans Club dinner in Orlando where he was the guest speaker. She was introduced to Kelly by George Robertson, a former Kelly aide. She was twenty-one and a twice divorced mother of a three-year-old son. I was to learn that several months later she saw Kelly at a wedding reception in Orlando and discussed the possibility of working for him. After he was elected, she was hired in a district office in Florida and had easy access to Kelly by being assigned his driver when he was scheduled to be in the district.

The early years in Washington were stressful for me and the children. Some of this would have been expected along with the excitement of it all, but we had the added burden of dealing with the unexpected. The children were adjusting to a new school and friends, the house needed to be put in order, my adjusting to a new life and finding my way in a new world, and still being very involved in the office and making appearances in Florida. This kept me in overload. But it was even worse than I knew.

How blessed was I to have connected so quickly with the support system that I would so soon need to weather this storm.

Many invitations came our way with being a part of the Ninety-fourth Congress; however, there was little joy in participating in these events in which relatively few have the opportunity.

Being in the House Chamber for the swearing in ceremony

Inaugural ceremony and ball

The State of the Union message in the House Chamber

"Members of the United States Senate and the House of Representatives request the pleasure of your company at the 23rd annual National Prayer Breakfast with The President of the United States and Mrs. Ford International Ballroom, Washington Hilton Hotel"

Sitting in the President's box at the Kennedy Center "Here at the Kennedy Center, Americans from all walks of life partake of some of the best creative work that our society has to offer. Mrs. Ford and I are pleased to make these tickets available to you with our best wishes for a most enjoyable occasion."

An evening on the presidential yacht, the Sequoia

Welcome Aboard Air Force One, Congressman Kelly

Christmas Ball at the White House

Easter egg hunt on the White House grounds

Special tours of the White House for our friends

Nelson Rockefeller was the first Vice President to have an official home located at the United States Naval Observatory, and we were invited

"Republican Congressional wives 'brown-bagged' it yesterday on the White House lawn as guests of Betty Ford. Mrs. Ford, a member for twenty-five years, had discussed inviting the club to the White House when she attended the January meeting.

"I might have to ask you to brown-bag it. With inflation, my husband is after me to cut down." *The Washington Star*, June 19, 1975. She said that she had never hosted the club before because her house was too small.

Being a part of the Congressional Wives Club

Attending the First Ladies Luncheon, and so much more

These occasions were attended and appreciated but done so with a heavy heart.

The relationship apparently had grown without my knowledge until the phone call about trouble on its way. Judy Foley then became a personal problem and a bitter campaign issue.

This brings to mind the advice given the new congressional wives during orientation: "No matter if the congressman is short, plump, bald, and with a wart on his nose, there will be a miniskirt chasing him."

I could not have handled this alone. When my life began to unravel, I could not have had a better support group: Joanne Kemp, Ellen Armstrong, Dr. Halverson, and Mary Glynn Peeples.

Dr. Richard Halverson was the pastor of the Fourth Presbyterian Church which I attended after Kelly left home. He later served as the chaplain of the senate. He was available to me 24/7. His constant advice was: Do not close the door. Keep the door open. Love and compassion could show him the way back home.

Kelly was to later say that he wished he had met Dr. Halverson sooner. His choices would have been different.

Ellen Armstrong, wife of Bill Armstrong from Colorado, chose to be my big sister when I arrived in Washington and was a member of Joanne Kemp's Friday study group. At Joanne's invitation, I also became a member in 1975. This group of believers became my Washington family.

Antoinette Hatfield, wife of the Oregon senator, told me early on not to expect any deep friendships while in Washington. This certainly was not to be my experience.

Campus Crusade had purchased a home on Embassy Row to serve as a Christian Embassy for members of Congress. A friend, Marie Miller, had asked me to help with decorating this beautiful home. Mary Glynn and Sam Peeples had just returned from the Philippines where they had served as missionaries with Campus Crusade. Their new assignment was the Congress: Sam for the men and Mary Glynn for the women. When the house was ready, Vonette Bright and I hosted the first luncheon for the wives of the new congressmen. Vonette and Bill Bright, founder of Campus Crusade, and Mary Glynn and Sam hosted an evening meeting with the new members of Congress. Kelly and I were there.

Mary Glynn and I had become sisters in Christ. Her advice was to let Kelly hit bottom. "He must, before he can come up again." She felt that I was enabling him by keeping my silence and covering for him. Often there are examples of a life wrecked before it is saved—Chuck Colson being one.

During this time, Kelly was not living at home when he received a call at his congressional office in Washington that his mother had died. He called and asked if I would take care of it. His mother was cremated, and the ashes were sent to him.

With Kelly's assurance that the affair was over and that he wanted to put our life back together, I went to Florida and helped with the campaign to get him reelected in 1976. We attended our home church in the district, and as we were leaving, our minister greeted us and said to Kelly, "I would not have given you a wooden nickel's chance of winning if Loraine had not come with you."

Jimmy Carter was elected president that November 2, 1976, defeating Gerald Ford. We attended the inauguration.

For Loraine Kelly, Best Wishes — Rosalynn Carter

A poll paid for by Kelly showed him with a wide lead in April 1978. This poll was conducted while Kelly was getting headlines for a visit to Cuba from November 22 to December 4. Sherri went with him on this trip and received gifts from Castro of four dozens of red roses and a tortoise shell necklace and bracelet. He must have been impressed by this young and pretty blonde American who could speak with him in Spanish.

Kelly paid $7,000 for the poll and agreed only to release the results of the Fifth District election matches and his rating. The poll also asked about issues and other politicians in the state, but Kelly refused to reveal that data.

Kelly told me that one of the questions he asked was: If he divorced me, would it defeat him? The poll caused him to think it would not.

The *Washington Star* reported "he was under fire for bringing a pretty secretary from his Florida office to Washington with a doubled salary. His wife rallied around to help him keep his seat in 1976, but after the election, he divorced her and married the young lady."

"Mrs. Kelly continues to maintain her silence on the Foley matter." It all happened so quickly. I kept my silence believing that this too will pass and believing that the least said less to mend. Also, the children were to be considered. Our marriage had not been tested in this way. Upon reflection, I'm not so sure that keeping my silence was the best decision. At the same time, Kelly was telling the children that I was out to ruin him if I exposed him.

The *Orlando Sentinel* reported, "Another political problem may arise for Kelly from his announcement July 11 that he will divorce his wife, Loraine. Kelly's private life became an issue two years ago when a month before the November 1976 General Election, Kelly's Democratic opponent, JoAnn Saunders, charged that newspapers were "withholding information" about an alleged relationship between Kelly and one of his staff secretaries.

It was being reported that there was no connection between the pending divorce and rumors about Kelly's relationship with the secretary.

I refused to give him a divorce. If he wanted it, he must get it. Kelly filed for divorce July 15, 1977, and called a news conference to make the announcement.

When Kelly called to tell me what he had done, he suggested that I might want to get out of town for a few days to avoid the press. The children and I drove to the Eastern Shore of Maryland. A few things were hurriedly packed for a few days away to think about where we could go from here. We could only stay and eat where credit cards were taken—no thought was given to getting cash. It was near Sherri's birthday, and wanting to be as upbeat as possible for them, we went to a boardwalk auction. Sherri was to choose an item to bid on as her present. She chose and bid on a colorful, happy painting of a woman and children with balloons on a beach celebrating. She got her painting and John also bid on one and got his.

When I returned home in McLean, I called Charlotte and John Briggs in Jacksonville, and they asked that we come to them. They were very supportive and could not believe what was happening. John talked with Kelly, but his decision had been made, and there was no turning back.

Kelly was granted a divorce without my being there on a Saturday, May 8, 1978, in St. Petersburg. The *Gainesville Sun* reported April 16, 1978, "Mrs. Kelly and the congressman have been separated at least since last July, when he filed for a divorce in a St. Petersburg court."

"I was disturbed by the knowledge that Pasco County's former judge had changed wives after he went to Washington, ditching a sharp, politically astute woman for a former secretary half his age." (Commentary by Lucy Morgan, *St. Petersburg Times*)

After denying any relationship or hopes for one, Judy Foley and Kelly were married in November, 1978. He called on Thanksgiving Day to give me and the children the news.

11

THE DOWNFALL CONTINUES

An American tragedy

John was home from Florida Central Academy near Orlando. Kelly insisted that he go to boarding school. He was sixteen. This was not a good experience for John. At home, he was sleeping on the floor at the foot of my bed thinking that I might leave him too. Sherri was in her senior year at McLean High School and was hoping for an early admission to Duke University. She was waitlisted there but was accepted at Vanderbilt. She said that I could not afford Vanderbilt—she should go to a less expensive college. My answer to her was that I couldn't afford not to send her; if the same should happen to her, she would be better prepared than I was. I altered my clothes for her and mortgaged my car, and she was on her way, eventually earning an MBA at the Darden School, University of Virginia.

Kelly's calling a news conference to announce our divorce was another "served me well." I now needed a way to support myself and the children. Jack Kemp and Ethel Kennedy were the first to call.

Jack Kemp, congressman from New York and husband of Joanne, talked with me about going across the country to help put together an organization for his presidential bid. "I want you to do for me what you did for Richard Kelly," he said. This was my cup of tea, but I could not take this on and take care of the children. They were my first priority.

A friend of mine had lunch with a friend of Ethel Kennedy, and they were discussing "what a mess Mrs. Kennedy's life was in." Senator Kennedy had just announced his candidacy for the office of president of the United States and had named Ethel Kennedy, his sister-in-law, his official hostess. My friend offered, "I have a friend who can put order in her life, if she will do it." They did not tell me. Mrs. Kennedy called night after night, until I agreed to meet and discuss what she wanted me to do for her.

We agreed to meet for coffee at Hickory Hill. It was evident she needed help. She first told me that she had fired her decorator and asked if I would redecorate Hickory Hill for the upcoming campaign. I knew the Kennedys owned the Merchandise Mart in Chicago; therefore, this could be a fun job, tailor-made for me. A book could be written about this experience.

I needed a job, and Hickory Hill was located very close to my home in Franklin Park, McLean, Virginia. This would work well for taking care of the children. I had told Mrs. Kennedy that my children had to come first. "Loraine Kelly now working for Robert Kennedy's Widow" was the headline in the papers.

Saturday, February 2, 1980, was the night that the news of Abscam broke on NBC television. After a long day at Hickory Hill, I had gone upstairs to get ready for bed and had turned the television on to hear the unbelievable story. My first thought was for the children. I immediately called Sherri at Vanderbilt to give her some notice of this breaking story, and we talked about how she might handle it. Kelly's being a part of Abscam was contrary to everything we had known about him. This was yet another blow to me and the children. We were adjusting to the divorce and now another trial.

The next day, Sunday, February 3, 1980, the headline of The *Washington Post* was "FBI 'Sting' Snares Several in Congress."

Abscam became public when details of an ongoing FBI investigation were leaked to the media. The leak was later attributed to the chief Abscam prosecutor. The leak made public that an FBI undercover Arab Scam "sting" operation, involving phony, oil-rich Arab sheiks with suitcases full of cash, stolen artwork, payoffs for Atlantic City casino licenses, and backroom influence peddling, was set up to catch organized crime figures selling stolen securities and art objects. By the end of the FBI's operation, they had also snared several members of Congress on potential bribery charges.

Immediate public reaction was found in the FBI files, asking "who" and "why" these particular congressmen were offered bribes. They were also asking if this were an effort by someone in the FBI or if someone was orchestrating the FBI to force Congress to knuckle under to the FBI's "clout." Members of Congress also had questions, knowing that the FBI was duty bound to protect them. The FBI was also asked if congressmen were chosen at random to accept the bribes or if they were selected due to their reputation. Kelly's reputation through previous trials could have made him a target, but there was nothing in his background that would have suggested that he would have taken a bribe. He had been vetted through trials before, and his integrity had never been questioned.

Mrs. Kennedy was traveling but sent flowers with a note:

> We may be campaigning but that doesn't mean we aren't thinking about you! Take as much time off as you like.

The sting, known as Abscam for Arab scam, came after Kelly and I were divorced. He was obsessed with writing a book about this nightmare. I can now understand why. He had asked me and many others—including Lucy and Richard Morgan—to help him, but they did not have the time. I could not then either, but now I should include this trial for him and his legacy and for the children. If truth be told, I think separating me from him was part of the plan of the FBI. Kelly certainly helped them with that. It was known that I covered Kelly's back, and it had often been reported over the years that I was the only one he trusted. Therefore, it could have been thought that removing me would make entrapment easier. Entrapping him was not easy; it took work.

One could have thought Kelly to have been a most unlikely candidate for the FBI to target. He was a former Marine, a prosecutor, and for thirteen years a trial judge. Kelly was a straight arrow who had demonstrated little appetite for the fancy lifestyle of Washington. His spending habits seemed every bit as conservative as his voting record: accumulative 95 ACU record during five years in the House. The only vulnerability could have been Kelly's standing with the party establishment. He was not a national party organization man. He was considered an outsider. He had been elected without the party establishment. This did not win him any favors.

Kelly struggled with the decision to leave his family, moving out and then back to our home more than a dozen times. The ultimate decision was made when he received a call that Judy had cut her wrists and was in the hospital. She may have had personal reasons for entering our lives, but she became a significant player in the entrapment. What were her reasons for trying to commit suicide? Interestingly, this never appeared in the newspapers. Who could I have gone to with that information, and how might it have affected the outcome? She had accepted my help twice when given the opportunities to leave for a better life. My guess was that her job had not been finished.

It was not long after I was out of the picture when there was news that loyal and trusted staff members, who had come to Washington with us, were let go. At the first opportunity, I asked Kelly about this. He said that he had a new manager in the office and felt he should take his recommendation for helpers.

J. P. Maher III (pronounced Marr) was hired on January 1, 1979, having come with a glowing letter of recommendation from U.S. Representative Margaret Heckler of Massachusetts, even though she had reasons for not putting him on her permanent staff. Maher put Kelly in the midst of

Abscam and introduced him to every "shady character" who took part in his downfall.

On February 3, the day after the news of the Abscam investigation leaked, Kelly contacted Nick Stames, assistant director of the FBI in charge of identification, for help in reaching Abscam investigators at the FBI. Stames was a street agent in Miami when Kelly worked with the U.S. attorney's office there. The FBI is charged with protecting members of Congress. Kelly was reaching out for that help. He later learned that the FBI had caused his office to be infiltrated by an informer or took advantage of a situation created by "powers known to the Justice Department."

"What led the FBI to focus on Kelly?" was the headline in the *Zephyrhills News*, Feb. 14, 1980.

The better question would be "*Who* led the FBI to focus on Kelly?" The best answer could come from the establishment, believing that they could not get him down there, get him up there for them. Interestingly, long-time members of Congress from Florida who were most certainly involved with the establishment did not seek reelection in 1974 after Kelly was elected.

Couple the establishment connection with the fact that for three terms, Kelly had preached bootstrap conservatism, railing just as strongly against wage and price controls and federal loan guarantees to Chrysler and New York City as he did against welfare cheats and food stamps, could explain the Carter administration labeling him a "troublemaker." This could be the *why*.

A big blow came for Kelly when he resigned in tears from the conference of all House Republicans to avoid the pain of a vote to expel him for alleged involvement in the Abscam bribery operation. This action came even before any charges had been brought. Representative Henry Hyde of Illinois described the action to expel as a "lynching." Some other members expressed concern for Kelly's due process rights, and others were concerned that they were moving too quickly. Representative Ed Bethune had a chance to wind up the debate. "Due process is not at stake here. What we are talking about are privileges, not rights. It is a privilege to sit in this conference, not a right. You speak of precedents being set. You are right. It is time to set precedents." Setting the precedent of finding one guilty before due process? Congressman William Whitehurst "memorialized" Ed Bethune's remarks in his book as a "ringing statement that defined the debate in a way that no one else had." The quote in the book began with, "This is not a criminal trial. It is not a court," yet Kelly was judged guilty even before any charges had been brought. The House Republicans were too quick to judge. They will now know the rest of the story.

Could it be that they chose to protect themselves in an election year even if it meant loss of honor and decency—loyalty?

No such action was taken by the Democrats against their members, even though two had already been indicted.

The House of Representatives ethics panel hired a lawyer for a bribery probe and began hearing evidence in this case in February. Witnesses were still being called at the end of May. It was noted that prosecutorial momentum was such that only the attorney general could have prevented an indictment at that point. Such action by what William Safire called "Jimmy Carter's Department of Political Justice seems highly unlikely."

The neat political symmetry of Abscam had attracted interest as noted in the *National Review* article dated June 27, 1980, "The Curious Case of Rep. Kelly":

> Out of the eight congressional targets of federal prosecution, exactly eight had been on the outs with the Administration in recent months: some of them had openly supported President Carter's political opponent, Edward Kennedy. Equally conspicuous was the fact that only one Republican was named—Kelly. Had there been eight Democrats, of course, the Abscam case could have been an election-year bombshell, a Democratic scandal. Thus the case against Kelly carried unique political significance.

The charges against Kelly were brought as the Republican Convention convened in Detroit and in the midst of his reelection campaign. That demonstrated its principal political purpose.

The Justice Department made a great show of wanting to find and discipline those who leaked word of the allegations to gain massive publicity. Yet, with criminal charges filed against the victims of the leaks, no immediate actions were taken as to the identity or motive of those who started the publicity campaign.

Maher introduced Kelly to a series of convicted felons in the summer and fall of 1979, telling him that they were legitimate businessmen who could help him with his 1980 political campaign.

Over time, Kelly became suspicious of Maher and wanted to fire him, but he feared political repercussions from Florida newspapers that were writing stories about his office staff turnover. Firing Maher would have involved the termination of eight other staffers whom Maher hired. He would have been expected to come up with a fairly substantial explanation for the firings, and he did not have one. Kelly felt that if Maher were in fact involved, as he believed him to be, he had to get more information.

Events had not come into focus yet. Kelly knew that he could be dumped out of office just as easily for being involved with criminals. He had no choice but to go forward. Maher continued encouraging him to get involved in financial dealings with men Kelly later learned were even more convicted felons.

Kelly never considered telling friends or other congressmen about this plight, believing that his life depended on his keeping the situation confidential. He felt it was important to play along and find out what kind of operation he was dealing with and why this extensive operation was aimed at him. The House ethics panel lawyer during the bribery probe asked the condemning question about his not even telling his wife (Judy) about conducting his own investigation. By then he must have had reasons for not trusting her.

Kelly's investigation consisted of this and this alone: to hold his course, to try and protect himself, and find out what these people were doing and why they wanted him. He was not an influential member of Congress. He was in the wrong party and was a relatively new member.

In Kelly's case, a judge would have to decide two basic issues: whether the conduct of the agenda was so "outrageous" that it violated the constitutional due process rights available to all criminal defendants and whether Kelly was entrapped.

Kelly found that he was appearing with people he would never have associated with in his life, their paths would never have crossed, and all of a sudden "I'm swimming in them." He was having lunch with paroled drug smugglers and gun dealers, going to a campaign barbecue at the home of another felon, rubbing elbows with cocaine dealers, discussing a business deal with a former federal prison inmate, and contracting for campaign work with yet another ex-convict living in Tarpon Springs under an assumed name.

Kelly said that he was totally unaware of where this thing began and where it ended. He didn't meet these people in a bar or at the race track or in a smoke-filled room, but in broad daylight upon the introduction of a trusted staff member, who had been highly recommended by a member of Congress.

Doubts about Maher and the men around him grew slowly, almost imperceptibly.

Kelly later learned that J. P. Maher had acted as a government informant in the past. Maher had been involved with the Justice Department in drug cases on three prior occasions. No wonder the Justice Department failed to warn Kelly about Maher. He was working for them.

In July 1980, after an exhaustive investigation of virtually every activity in Kelly's three terms in office and talking about it for six months, a grand jury indicted U.S. Representative Richard Kelly for bribery, conspiracy, and interstate travel to promote unlawful acts. Unbelievable!

In a blast at the Justice Department, Kelly immediately called the indictment "a grossly cynical manipulation of the criminal justice system for political ends."

Kelly said, "Based on my four years [of] experience as a federal prosecutor, there was no reason why the government could not have indicted me within ten days after January 8, the day accused of accepting a bribe, or February 2, the day news of Abscam leaked out, had the prime motive been justice."

Kelly pled innocent in July 1980, formally denying bribery and conspiracy charges against him, and then demanded that the Justice Department release all Abscam files that related to him.

Disclosure of the files was necessary so that Florida voters would have the entire story before that year's election. Kelly made the request in a letter that was hand delivered to President Carter at the White House at the same moment he was appearing in court denying the charges against him.

In a follow-up press release, Kelly wrote:

Mr. President, it is too late in this matter for your administration to retreat sanctimoniously behind the courts, or court procedures, as an excuse for failing to disclose before the election the whole truth. The Department of Justice has gone public against an elected member of Congress in an election year with a distorted, partial, and untrue publication which they blamed on someone else and called a "leak." I now, on behalf of the public, request and demand that a full disclosure of all information be made immediately.

The will of the people as expressed through the ballot is the essence of our United States Government. Consequently, the voice of the people is only as valid as the knowledge which they possess.

Kelly knew that the "dirty work" of the Justice Department leaks could not await the normal discovery process of the courts because of his pending election.

This announcement came just after prosecutors asked U.S. district court judge William B. Bryant to issue a protective order that would prohibit Kelly from disclosing information turned over to his lawyers by prosecutors before his trial. Prosecutors were willing to turn over evidence in the case if Kelly were willing to sign an agreement "limiting public disclosure" of the information.

Prosecutors cited, as grounds for the request, a *St. Petersburg Times* story that quoted Kelly saying he would share any information he received with the public.

Kelly said that the government should have thought about this before they went through the leaking process. The leaks were not a single episode; the government did it on an ongoing basis, divulging selective parts of this case.

Kelly, acting as his own attorney, went to federal court to charge that FBI agents went after him because the Carter administration considered him a "troublemaker." In a motion filed in the U.S. district court, Kelly said that he could prove that Assistant Attorney General Philip Heymann had said we had gotten the troublemaker in a conversation February 2, the day the news of the bribery scandal leaked out. This conversation occurred in the Brooklyn office of the Justice Department's Organized Crime Strike Force on the day FBI agents were making the rounds to notify the congressmen who were about to be publicly implicated in the Abscam operation. Heymann's office in Washington refused to comment on the allegation. Kelly was prepared to produce a witness who would substantiate the following conversation:

Unidentified questioner: Did we get Kelly?

Heymann: Yes, we got the troublemaker Kelly.

Kelly made the accusations in a motion that asked Judge Bryant to dismiss bribery and conspiracy charges against him on the ground that he was "selectively prosecuted."

Kelly believed he was targeted by the Carter administration because he had consistently opposed Carter's policies and had "focused the truth" on Carter's proposals brought before subcommittees on which he sat. He particularly made himself an enemy during a subcommittee meeting when he forced Carter's economic adviser Alfred Kahn to admit that the voluntary wage and price guidelines proposed by the president as the centerpiece of his war on inflation would not affect the government's fiscal or monetary policies. Federal loan guarantees for Chrysler Corporation were also opposed on the ground that the guarantees would provide excessive pay raises for autoworkers already overpaid. "In both of those instances, my efforts were made to focus the blazing light of truth on what was being done. And I can tell you that this system would not continue as it is, if more truth were told."

This highly publicized Abscam bribery trial began December 4, 1980. Kelly called me that morning to say that this was the first trial without me and that he was missing me. I wished him well.

The *St. Petersburg Times* noted that the trial would center on Kelly's believability that he had accepted $25,000 in cash not as a bribe but as part of his ongoing "investigation" of "shady characters." Suspecting he was under surveillance by them, he used one of the marked $100 bills to buy a hamburger at McDonald's to reassure the bribers, presumably, that he was "hooked." He returned the change to his office cache. He made no move to convert or wash the money. It was all in place when he called the FBI to reclaim it on February 3.

Those who had known Kelly believed him with no reservations. Of course, they would have had some history of his life. They would have lived the trials before this one and would have known him to be a straight arrow. If one had not, it is understandable that they would have doubts about his conducting his own investigation, not knowing that he was eminently qualified to do so and had no other choice.

Kelly's good friend since law school Anthony "Tony" Battaglia was his lawyer. He said that he viewed his defense of Kelly as a privilege. "There is no greater honor to be bestowed on a lawyer than to be called on to defend a fellow lawyer and congressman who he believes is telling the truth when he says he was conducting his own investigation." He felt that "Destiny called on me to do it." Their friendship had been cemented long ago in watermelon patches.

In setting the stage for Kelly's trial during the opening statements, Battaglia dubbed the FBI operation "The Abscam Circus" and divided the players into two "rings," with Weinberg as the principal performer and FBI Agent Amaroso as the "ringmaster." Detailing the "acts" of the circus, he said Weinberg and the FBI had added a new act—the buying of congressmen.

Almost all of the other evidence introduced during the trial was blotted out by a videotape showing Kelly taking $25,000 from an FBI undercover agent on January 8. The tape shown to the jury became the convicting evidence in this manufactured crime. A picture is worth a thousand words. It would be impossible to erase.

FBI undercover special agent Anthony Amoroso, who used the name Tony DeVito, was credited with roping Kelly into the investigation; it was recorded he wanted at least one Republican to balance off the number of Democratic Abscam defendants. He met with Weinberg and Ciuzio to discuss getting Kelly to introduce a private immigration bill in return for payment. Amoroso conceded that he had "conned" informants and middlemen in the case with offers of lavish salaries and expenses. He made seven specific offers of money to Kelly to sponsor legislation to allow a fictitious sheik to immigrate to the United States. "Federal investigators continued to ask U.S. Representative Richard Kelly to accept a bribe because they thought he was being 'cute' when he initially did not accept their offer."

No such legislation was ever introduced, and the offers of money were refused. The records show that Kelly had no alternative but to investigate the "shady characters" and had taken the money as evidence, which was returned.

Kelly was then accused of accepting the money as part of an agreement to assist a foreign national with immigration problems, even though providing immigration assistance was routinely extended to constituents free of charge.

Judge Bryant repeatedly criticized the conduct of the FBI and had said he found some of their actions to have been "outrageous." He did, however, have reservations about Kelly's claim that he accepted a $25,000 payment while conducting his own investigation of suspicious persons. Kelly said he ultimately accepted the money in an effort to find out what the men in the Georgetown house operated by FBI agents really wanted with him. He felt it was important to play along to get answers. When Kelly looked around and realized that he was surrounded by convicted felons and no help for him was coming from the FBI, he had no choice but to do his own investigation. He had the experience to do so; he had been a federal prosecutor. He had been one of their best and had been proud of it.

Newspaper reporters called for my reaction regarding this claim. I told them that this was standard operating procedure for Kelly and consistent with his life's work. Absolutely, I knew this claim to be true. Even a former law partner testified that this was true Kelly. It bothers me knowing that the outcome could have been different if I had been in the picture to document this transaction as I had always done during our marriage. Who could he have trusted? The FBI was duty bound to protect him. They were instead trying to ruin him. Why wouldn't he want to know who and why?

Making sense of this trial was much like putting the many pieces of a puzzle together. I could not have imagined and did not want to believe what I was finding in the records. I did not want to believe that this could happen to anyone in America, that one could be destroyed by selective prosecution and labeling them a "troublemaker" for taking a stand on issues he believed in. Wasn't this what he was elected to do? *And* for the need of a token Republican.

The chief Abscam prosecutor, Thomas P. Puccio, came dangerously close to getting entangled in the web of deceit woven to snag others. He turned his investigators who were con artists loose and let them run at large. Jack Anderson in his column for the *Washington Post* first praised the FBI undercover men and scathed the members of Congress who took their bribes. He was out front for the FBI and was ready to stay with them in reporting the good work they were doing. In digging deeper for follow-up stories about the case, Anderson was shocked at discovering what he called the "dirty work" being done by the FBI. The tables then turned when he exposed the FBI. Anderson soon learned that Puccio was preparing a smear story to discredit him. "Public apathy is the bane of democracy. Repetition is its cure." Anderson began hammering away unremittingly about the FBI's misconduct in his newspaper columns. The Abscam case then began to crumble.

"It has an odor to it that's going to be cleared before anybody gets convicted. It has an odor to it that is absolutely repulsive," Chief Judge William B. Bryant told the lawyers, according to a court transcript.

Deputy Attorney General Charles Renfrew and FBI Director William Webster had now recommended two prosecutors and about five FBI agents be disciplined for the news leaks about Abscam and other undercover probes.

A few of the "shady characters" introduced to Kelly by J. P. Maher for this lynching will be named for some understanding of why Kelly was driven in his pursuit of justice. Anyone would have done the same if found caught in the same web. In this case he had no other choice but to seek out the truth on his own.

J. P. Maher, who Kelly believed to be a trusted aide, had acted as a government informant in the past and was a convicted felon. He was arrested in Bolivia on cocaine charges and had admitted his background in drug smuggling. He was associated with the convicted felons involved and had introduced every one of them to Kelly.

Melvin Weinberg, an informer for the FBI since 1960 and a convicted New York con man who dreamed up the Abscam circus, was paid $138,000 by the FBI for his services. He agreed to set up the sting to avoid going to prison. He was caught in a securities fraud and sentenced to three years. The FBI engineered his release and promoted him to the payroll as an employee. Abscam was a con man's dream come true, because now he could do it legally. Weinberg described Abscam as a honeypot to catch flies. The FBI even raised his pay and bonuses, which were substantial when he asked for more. Weinberg was quoted as saying about Abscam,

"I couldn't believe what was going on. If we get away with this, we can get away with anything."

Weinberg's wife, Marie, introduced damaging evidence about her husband's relationship with the FBI in an affidavit prepared in 1982. Marie accused her husband of intentionally engaging in conduct that entrapped Kelly. It was recorded that Weinberg hounded her—and FBI agents joined in the harassment—until she reportedly committed suicide. She was found hanging by the neck in an empty condo in Florida. I believe she had help in causing her death. It had been announced that she was scheduled to appear on national television the following week to tell her story.

William Rosenberg, already a convicted felon, was part of a chain of people leading undercover agents to Kelly. Rosenberg was found guilty in July 1980 of conspiracy to bribe Kelly.

Eugene Ciuzio, a Longwood business consultant, was noted for attempts to con the con artists, saying he lied when he told Weinberg about a relationship with Kelly in an effort to convince them that he could really produce congressmen for Abscam. He said he was just "puffing" when he said Kelly would accept a bribe, later saying, "Kelly is a hell of a guy. He's the most honest guy I ever met. I know the truth, he's innocent."

Stanley Weisz, a New York accountant, was acting as middleman with Ciuzio to get Kelly to accept a $25,000 payment from an undercover FBI agent. Weisz thought he had stumbled into an unbelievable fantasy world when he accepted $50,000 "just for introducing two people."

Ciuzio and Weisz were convicted of helping bribe Kelly and traveling across state lines to help in the bribery.

Joseph F. Valverde, disbarred New York lawyer Samuel Glasser, and J. P. Maher were classmates at Cornell University in the 1960s. Valverde, Glasser, and Michaelson were convicted of crimes in New York. Robert Michaelson, a Long Island businessman who met Glasser in prison, attempted to sign Kelly as a business partner.

Prosecutors labeled Kelly's lone investigation as a "desperation defense" as closing arguments got under way in Kelly's bribery trial, and asked, "Is this an investigation or a sham?"

Battaglia, "choking with emotion" as he concluded, begged the jurors to see that "Richard Kelly is not guilty" and accused the FBI of being the only real criminals involved in Abscam.

Kelly's lawyer: His job is done, and now he waits

Anthony S. Battaglia has done everything he can to convince a Washington jury that Kelly did not take a bribe.

By LUCY MORGAN
St. Petersburg Times Staff Writer   1-25-81

· WASHINGTON — The words of an Irish ballad flow from the lips of a stocky Italian-American who is standing in the middle of the Dubliner, a crowded Irish bar that attracts the Capitol Hill crowd.

The singing Italian is Anthony S. Battaglia, a St. Petersburg lawyer who has donated a year of his 53-year life to an old law school classmate who has managed to get himself into a bad scrape.

The classmate is Florida's former U.S. Rep. Richard Kelly and this night in the Dubliner is special for Battaglia.

In the glare of TV lights, Kelly (left) is helped to his car by lawyer Anthony

In the glare of TV lights, Kelly (left) is helped to his car by lawyer Anthony Battaglia, AP photo, as reported by Lucy Morgan, St. Petersburg Times , 1-8-81

Kelly, when asked how he felt now that the trial was going to the jury: I feel detached. I think I've spent so much time in court, I look upon it as a process and I think the process is good. I have confidence it. You know it's human, so it's not perfect.

On January 27, 1981, the word rang out across the federal courtroom: Kelly guilty in Abscam.

It takes a bigger man than most for Kelly to say after the verdict: I'm not in any way unhappy with the system. I love my government, I love the people, and I respect the process—it is man who corrupts it.

On November 4, 1981, Kelly appealed the verdict. Will the judge go with the jury or throw Kelly verdict out? The judge must decide two basic issues: whether the conduct of the agents were so "outrageous" that it violated the constitutional due process right available to all criminal defendants and whether Kelly was entrapped. Another report put it this way: the judge must decide which outweighs the other—a government investigation that had been described as riddled with misconduct or a U.S. congressman who took the witness stand in his courtroom and told a "fantastic" tale of conducting his own investigation.

On May 15, 1982, Kelly's trial verdict was reversed: 1 Abscam Conviction Overturned. Throughout the trial, Judge Bryant, often in colorful language, had condemned the Abscam tactics and seemed on the verge of dismissing the case, only to overrule defense motions. His distaste for many aspects of the case was evident by not only his words but also by his expressions, it was reported. Judge Bryant had said that this case had an odor to it.

Judge William B. Bryant had found that Kelly's rights were violated. He said that law enforcement exceeds its bounds when it manufactures crimes and creates criminals. A person corrupted under circumstances which only police officials can create or by a process which only the authorities are licensed to use had been made into a criminal by his own government. Almost no one can regard the Abscam trap as anything but odious. The very "characters" involved proved to be less than admirable, and few could deny that

Kelly had reasons to be "suspicious" of them and was driven to investigate them.

Kelly was quoted as saying that he couldn't rejoice in Bryant's decision because the entire Abscam episode was sad for the nation. We need the FBI and need to believe in them. Kelly said that the FBI just did a super job in snookering everybody.

More than a dozen Tampa Bay citizens whose lives had been touched by Kelly took the witness stand during his trial as character witnesses. Most of the witnesses were a part of Kelly's life during his days as a federal prosecutor and circuit judge and therefore knew him well.

Joe McClain, a Dade City attorney and former state representative once said that he was "humiliated" by Kelly; this was a charge in Kelly's impeachment. When McClain, about five feet seven, showed up in Court without a coat; Kelly, who stood six feet four, furnished his famous spare. The incident occurred because Kelly believed that for the same reason he wore a robe, a lawyer should wear a coat when doing serious business affecting lives before the court. Even so, McClain testified that he had never heard anyone question Kelly's honesty before.

St. Petersburg lawyer Barney Masterson and Tampa lawyer Michael Kinney, the men who defended Kelly when his conduct as a judge was challenged by the Judicial Qualifications Commission in 1968, described Kelly as a "remarkable man with great integrity." Former U.S. attorney John Briggs, then a Tampa lawyer, said that Kelly was scrupulously honest. John was best man at our wedding and the namesake of our son. Among those who testified that Kelly had a reputation for honesty and truthfulness above reproach were: U.S. Representative C. W. "Bill" Young, who was in the Florida senate during the Kelly impeachment trial; Citrus County newspaper editor David Arthurs; and Pasco County commissioner Sandra Werner. Kelly's former law partner, Lester Bales, said he guessed what he was doing in advance—that's 100 percent Kelly.

The injustice continued. In May 1983, an appeals court reinstated the 1981 jury verdict, and that decision sent Kelly back to Judge Bryant's courtroom. The U.S. Supreme Court refused to review the appellate decision in October.

Judge Bryant could have dismissed the case, or granted a new trial on the grounds that government attorneys had concealed evidence showing that he had been targeted by Abscam agents, or declared Kelly guilty and sentenced him to prison.

The new evidence was an affidavit filed in U.S. district court in Seattle by former government informer James Davenport, who was in prison at the time. Davenport attested that in 1980 he was asked by government agents to contact Melvin Weinberg, the FBI's chief informant in Abscam. At Weinberg's direction, he visited Kelly's office, pretending to offer assistance in Kelly's defense. While there, he stole papers relating to that case. In October 1980, Davenport sent a letter to the U.S. attorney's office in Washington from an Indiana jail. He offered information about Abscam and his visit with Kelly. FBI Agent Roy Carroll was sent to Indiana to interview him and later filed a report on that interview. But the U.S. attorney's office did not make the letter or the agent's report available to Kelly. This information would have been used as substantive evidence of entrapment.

Other new evidence was the affidavit prepared by Weinberg's wife, Marie. She was found dead a few days after she signed the affidavit. It accused Weinberg of intentionally engaging in conduct that entrapped Kelly.

Kelly contended this evidence was not available at his trial and should have established sufficient grounds for the Judge to order a new trial.

On January 13, 1984, the headline read, "Kelly gets 6 to 18 months in prison in Abscam case."

Judge Bryant sentenced Kelly just hours after rejecting defense arguments to acquit Kelly or grant a new trial. "I have sincere doubts about whether I am right or not [in denying Kelly's motions]. I think what the government did in this case brought about the downfall of a person who if left alone might well have lived out his life as a law-abiding citizen . . . No concept of fundamental fairness can accommodate what happened to Kelly. The FBI outrageously created a crime and entrapped him in it."

"I'm not unsympathetic with you," Bryant said as he ruled against Kelly. But he also declared that Kelly's story—that he accepted the bribe money only as part of his own investigation of suspicious people—was "nonsense" and said that he thought that story resulted in Kelly's conviction.

The Abscam trial was centered on Kelly's believability. Could Kelly convince a jury that he was conducting his own investigation when he took $25,000 from Abscam's undercover FBI agents? Apparently not; he was not believed by the jury and was not believed by the judge. "Judge Bryant was impressed with the moral integrity and virtue of Kelly, but he too decided to play the game."

Asked if he thought the sentence fair, Kelly answered, "If I'd been treated fairly and if I were guilty, I'd think it fair, but I wasn't. So I don't think it was fair."

Lucy Morgan reported that Kelly rejected a federal judge's offer to dismiss the charges against him if he would just claim entrapment. To do that, he would have been forced to admit guilt. He would not; instead, he chose prison.

He had done the same during the impeachment, the first trial. He was offered a deal, just move out of the county so business as usual could continue, and the charges would be dropped against him. He refused the deal.

When a life is at stake, couldn't one have chosen to give Kelly the benefit of the doubt in the case?

Eugene Patterson, editor of *St. Petersburg Times*, in an article, "A Question of Ethics" (January 15, 1984):

> Kelly had no criminal record. He did not have a bad reputation. How had they proved that he was predisposed, ready, and willing to commit the crime without hesitation? He was a law-abiding citizen and had served his country honorably.

This hard-hitting former Marine had been credited with being "more responsible than any other individual with cleaning up politics in Pasco County."

Five FBI agents and two Philadelphia prosecutors were sharply disciplined by the Justice Department for news leaks in the

THROUGH TRIALS TO GLORY

Abscam investigation and other federal probes. It confirmed "the unhappy truth that some employees of this department violated the rules." They manufactured crimes and created criminals.

James Neal, counsel to the senate's committee, questioned Mullen intensely on the FBI's use of convicted con man Melvin Weinberg as a central figure in the investigation. "Here's a man who's had twenty-five years as a cheat, a liar . . . Here's a man you could not control," said Neal, chief Watergate trial lawyer. Neal established during questioning that the FBI had used Weinberg as an informant until the mid-1970s when he was dropped after the bureau learned he was conducting an independent scam on the side.

"You need a Mel Weinberg to start one of these operations," Mullen responded. "You need the instant credibility . . . We do it all the time. We control them as best we can. We're aware going into it that they're not Boy Scouts. It's a difficult issue, but it's something we must do if we're going to succeed."

Even so, the FBI defended their techniques at a senate hearing, saying the value of the Abscam investigation outweighed the problems.

From the FBI files, I found "Abscam was an enterprise that rewrote the books for FBI undercover operations." Did it take killing Kelly to bring about these changes? That was a mighty price to pay, but hopefully, it will save others.

If Abscam caused change for the better, at least Kelly's episode would not have been in vain. He had caused change for the better with every trial. This was the most costly. If it could happen to him, it could happen to any of us. If you do not believe that these things happen in America, read Harvey Silverglate's book *How the Feds Target the Innocent* and wake up.

Kelly served a ten-month prison sentence at Eglin Air Force Base in the Florida Panhandle in 1985–1986 and then spent three months in a St. Petersburg halfway house. An editorial noted that it was interesting that Representative Margaret Heckler went to Ireland as U.S. ambassador, and Kelly went to jail.

It was no wonder that Kelly was consumed with finding the answer to *who* was targeting him and *why* he was being targeted. He was hopeful when he read an article by Roland Manteiga in *La Gaceta* recapping his trial and then stating what Kelly thought to be true: If the government is free surreptitiously to bring about the downfall of any person it can induce to step off the straight and narrow path, who is going to be safe from the hidden camera eye?

It is easy to say that an honest citizen has nothing to fear. But when dishonest practices can be employed against him by his government in disguise, there is much to be feared.

Kelly, in a handwritten note to his daughter:

Dear Sherri,

This does not exculpate me from having been tempted but it does from crime. It is, however, a dramatic change in the attitude of this paper, and it is the first time fault has been found with the FBI. The only way the truth can be had is by a willingness to stop screaming at Kelly and look honestly and objectively at why the FBI was doing what they did. This will focus on how they did it, in truth, then the charge that I was tempted will be erased or at least in serious doubt by all.

Reuters:

A secretive U.S. Drug Enforcement Administration unit is funneling information from intelligence intercepts, wiretaps, informants and massive database of telephone records to authorities across the nation to help them launch criminal investigations of Americans.

The undated documents show that federal agents are trained to "recreate" the investigative trail to effectively cover up where the information originated, a practice that some experts say violates a defendant's constitutional right to a fair trial. If defendants don't know how an investigation began, they cannot know to ask to review potential sources of exculpatory evidence—information that could reveal entrapment, mistakes, or biased witnesses.

"It was an amazing tool," said one recently retired federal agent. "Our big fear was that it wouldn't stay secret."

Doesn't this fit Kelly's case? Kelly was quoted as saying that he was totally unaware of where this thing began or where it ended.

———————————

I've read that wrongful prosecution of innocent conduct twisted into a felony charge has wrecked many an innocent life and career. Now, I know this to be true. It also changes the entire tapestry of a family.

"Society will not support courageous politicians," Kelly wrote. The mediocre majority is destroying our heroes for their beliefs in one or two causes, rather than admiring the courage of a man willing to put all his worldly possessions on the line for his beliefs. What are we then left with—mediocrity—cowards?

Richard Morgan in the *St. Petersburg Times* called Kelly's downfall an American tragedy, regardless of what you may think. His fateful journey from the circuit court bench in Pasco County to a federal prison at Eglin Air Force Base is an American tragedy. "His fall from grace is especially disturbing to those of us who live in Pasco because he is a local personality. He lived in Zephyrhills and Holiday, served fourteen years as a judge in Dade City and New Port Richey and then represented the county in Congress for six years." He felt Kelly's disgrace keenly because Richard said he admired his performance as a judge, and he counted him as a friend. In 1968, he united Richard and Lucy in marriage in the old Westside courtroom in New Port Richey.

Judge Kelly went out of his way to see that the little person received a fair shake in his court. That's what first attracted Richard to him. He recalled a case in which he refused to proceed with a defendant who spoke little English until an interpreter could be located. The defendant's command of the language was insufficient to fully comprehend the case against him. Neither the state nor the defense shared that view, as Richard recalled, but Kelly was insistent that an interpreter be found. Eventually, one was.

Richard reported that Kelly was scrupulously ethical when it came to public funds and property. He refused to use the county's toll-free telephone line to call his home in Zephyrhills. He wouldn't use a county postage stamp to mail a personal letter. He was a stickler about things like that as a judge. He brought his own lunch and ate at his desk, often offering half of his sandwich to any visitor. He often described the desk in his chamber as the "people's desk."

Richard asked about Abscam, "Can we forget the sight of Kelly stuffing $25,000 in small bills into his coat pockets?" He thought more than anything else, that scene—forever on videotape—convicted Kelly of bribery. There's no way that a jury is going to disregard evidence that is so damning. He reported that Kelly accepted the money because he was conducting his own investigation of some suspicious activities. But his main defense was that he was entrapped by the FBI. I would reverse the two: When Kelly realized he was entrapped by the FBI, he was left with no other choice but to seek out the truth on his own. Richard had known Kelly as a judge and should have known that it would have been out of character for Kelly to take a bribe. How could $25,000 have made a difference in his life? Would he have risked all to buy a hamburger?

Richard Morgan agreed with the trial judge: the FBI's conduct was outrageous. But the jury found Kelly guilty. He was willing to let it go at that since they heard the evidence firsthand and he had not. The jury can get it wrong. The video obscured the other evidence. The difference was Richard Morgan knew Kelly and could have given him the benefit of the doubt; the jury did not, and neither did Judge Bryant.

What does the Bible say about trials? They will come. Life is tough, but God is good. Trials are not an opposition to our happiness but an opportunity for holiness and maturity that leads to true joy.

Judy Kelly told a reporter that "there won't be anything left untold" in her tell-all book, which she said "will provide details of their relationship" that began when she worked as a secretary for Kelly in 1975.

The reporter called to ask what I thought about Judy's decision to write a book. I responded that this was news to me.

Then I set about locating Judy. She was quite surprised to hear from me. I told her that I understood she was writing a book but for her to keep in mind that I knew the whole story and the truth. I also told her that I was only interested in what she did to the extent that it would affect my children.

She was already untruthful with her remarks during the affair: no relationship, no plans, and no marriage. During the 1974 campaign, Hazel

Croasdale, a very good friend and neighbor, and Doug Merrill, a young man who had given up his job for a year to campaign with us, tried to warn me about Judy. Kelly and I had such a strong marriage that had been tested from day one that it was hard for me to believe the news about an affair could be true.

There were so few hours in the day that we were not together during the campaign. Apparently they had information that I did not.

A test of good and bad choices is often the opportunity. The seduction began when Judy was assigned as Kelly's driver for scheduled appearances in the district. Kelly failed the test, and this weakened his position.

During our separation, Kelly kept telling me that he wanted to come home. What was holding him? I talked with Kelly about my helping Judy leave. He did not believe she would go but agreed for me to try. I gave her two opportunities to leave for a life better than what she ever had. It should be mentioned that she was living this clandestine life with a small son. He was about five at the time. She had been married twice already at this early age. She was about twenty-seven years younger than Kelly. Both times I offered her a way out, she took them. Arrangements were made for her and her son, and I promised to support her for a year. She left town, but she was back in no time.

I was told by a friend that Battaglia, Kelly's attorney and friend, had to insist that Judy appear with Kelly at the trial. Could it be that she felt that her job was done?

The suicide attempt sealed the deal. Kelly called a press conference to announce our divorce. I think he had to make it public because the indecision was killing him and all of us. I was no help. Taking Dr. Halverson's advice to leave the door open, I told him that I could forgive him, that I understood how this could happen. The children and I wanted him to come home.

He asked that I get the Bible and read to him what it said about what a wife should be. After reading it, he said, "You are everything it says you should be. The problem is not you—I am the problem." He had told me so many times, "The day I married you was the happiest day of my life."

When he came just before Abscam was leaked to ask if I would remarry him, I believe he was asking for my help. I did not know then that the FBI had just informed him that he would be named in Abscam.

If I had known, would I have responded differently?

12

A STORY WORTH TELLING

Lessons to be learned

Over the years I have often looked at the trunks that had been stored in the garage. They held every detail of these trials. I even thought about burning them. But destroying the information somehow would have said that we had fought the good fight in vain.

The Abscam part of the story is being told for the children and the record, but more importantly, it is for Richard Kelly. He believed that he was the victim of a well-orchestrated plot to destroy him. I believe the evidence proves that he was right. His remaining years were spent searching for as many details of the plot as he could, looking for justice, and struggling to live with the aftermath of the "bomb that went off in the middle of his life." He died not knowing why he had been targeted or by whom. Nothing in his life would have forecast the outcome.

His good friend Anthony "Tony" Battaglia knew him well and was quoted when he heard of Kelly's death: We loved one another. He was thought to be a very difficult man if you weren't close to him, but if you were close enough to learn what kind of mind he had, you loved him.

Kelly was a self-made man who set very high standards for himself even though he did not have the role models to emulate, which left some voids. There is no perfect person, but his voids contributed to his downfall. In spite of the voids, he experienced amazing accomplishments, considering his humble beginning.

He did have the good fortune of meeting Mr. and Mrs. Harris who had a winter home in Florida near the foster home. This relationship helped mold Kelly's character at a very early age. They were well educated and had a wonderful library and lifestyle they shared with Kelly. They wanted to adopt him, but he proudly remained a Kelly. Mr.

and Mrs. Harris offered everything they owned to him, but he declined. He only accepted Mr. Harris's ring but asked for a bill of sale as proof of the gift. The ring became my wedding ring. Kelly was considered a part of their family as long as they lived.

Sherri and John should know what a blessing they were in our lives and how much they contributed to the happy memories in "The Little House" in spite of the trials. They should be very proud of their dad who was the person they knew him to be.

And now there are grandchildren, and as they get older, they will want to know about the day when their grandparents walked that lonely road and made the decision to stand strong and tall for what was right, knowing full well there would be a mighty price to pay. We were strong as long as we were together.

It is believed that a midlife breakup affects the structure of the family for generations on the general premise that divorce breeds divorce. I challenge every member of my family to help break this cycle. When any one of you chooses a life partner, "until death do us part," be sure that the partner believes in God and that you care for that person more than yourself. Honor the commitment you made when you married. Always remember the love and dreams you had going into the marriage. You can be sure that rough times will come. There will be bumps in the road, but the measure of who you are is how you react to those hurdles. Working through these times will make your marriage stronger and you a better person. I could not resist telling Kelly that he won every election and won every trial while we were together. He lost the ones after the divorce. This supports the belief that a divided house will fall.

In the end, Kelly paid the price for being a maverick. To again quote Richard Morgan, *St. Petersburg Times*, "His detractors—and they are legion—doubtless will characterize his downfall as 'good riddance' and 'it's his own fault.'" No one believed that he was investigating his own case when he finally took the money, which he returned. But I knew him best, and this story about his life and the evidence proves that he was investigating the "shady characters" whose objective was to ruin him. There was nothing in his background that would ever have suggested otherwise. The investigation was "100 percent Kelly."

Kelly came back twice to ask me to remarry him. I can only think that he wanted me by his side during the tough times, as I had always been. I would have been that person who documented his investigation of the "shady characters," as I had always done. Much was reported about his not telling anyone. Who could he have trusted?

The second time Kelly asked me to remarry him was after he learned he had Alzheimer's. He wanted someone around who cared for him, but I had given everything I had to our marriage— there was no more to give—and he was married.

I chose not to consider remarrying after divorce because I wanted to fulfill my responsibilities to our children. They had lost their father; they were not losing me. Also, I knew that every move made by me would be woven into the tapestry of our lives. Breaking the cycle could begin with me.

Richard Kelly died in a nursing home in Stevensville, Montana, on August 22, 2005, without family and obscured by Abscam. This was the saddest day of my life. My last words to him shortly before he died were, "It was not all bad. We had two beautiful children together."

I had saved the handwritten note he had written to us when he left:

Dear Raine & Lil Guys,

Be good to each other. I'll look forward to seeing you soon.

Love,

R

13

BLESSINGS

My sufficiency

I'm reminded of a song I learned so long ago when our church youth group would sit around a campfire on the beach, roasting marshmallows, singing,

> God gave the wise men their wisdom and to the poets their dreams. To father and mother, their love for each other, but he left me out so it seems. I went around broken hearted, thinking life but an empty affair. But when God gave me you, it was then that I knew, he had given me more than my share.
>
> —Author Unknown

One of God's many gifts was surrounding me with people who loved the Lord. The four most involved in my life were Ellen, Joanne, Dr. Halverson, and Mary Glynn. There were others.

The first blessing was Ellen Armstrong's choosing to be my big sister. Then Ellen's taking me to Joanne's Friday group and being invited into what was to become my Washington family. What a great support system to have in Washington, where power rules and marriages fail.

Ellen drove me to every ladies event during my first year in Washington. We became good friends. I even stayed with Anne and Will, the Armstrong children, at times when Ellen and Bill would go back to their district in Colorado. It warms my heart still when I hear Anne call out "Mama Kelly" and remembering taking Will to Little League practices.

Joanne became more than a friend and mentor; she was our "mother hen." She truly cared and nurtured us in every way, especially in our spiritual growth. Her Friday group was mostly of other wives of members of Congress and those in high government positions who needed a safe haven to stay grounded in the Word. She remains private in protecting her purpose; her light shines.

The influence that she has had is wide spread and is most beautifully reflected in her children. The Kemp family allowed me into their family, and I am eternally grateful and blessed.

When divorce came for me, Joanne asked, "I don't want to put my head in the sand and think this can't happen to me. If it can happen to you, it can happen to me. What should I do differently?" I told her I thought I had done it right, but it didn't work. Jack had just asked her to accompany him to Brazil, but she felt she could not go because of their four children at home. This was to be her first trip out of the country. I told her to go, that I would move in and take care of Jeff, Jennifer, Judith, and Jimmy. I loved the time with them.

I last saw Jack Kemp in 2008 when I was invited to Washington for another eightieth birthday celebration with about twenty-five of the Friday group. Rosemary Boulter had booked a flight for me to attend. Members who were otherwise involved and could not attend the party Sherri gave at her home on Wildlife Drive, St. Simons Island, Georgia, so I was invited to go to them. Jeff was with Focus on the Family, and Jack had committed to be their speaker during a cruise. A big surprise that day was Jack's being home with the women when I arrived. He had sent his car and driver to fetch me from the Baltimore airport. What a wonderful birthday celebration with my Washington family.

A short time after this trip I was told by the doctor at the Mayo Clinic in Jacksonville that they could do nothing more for my cancer. A radical hyperthermic isolated limb perfusion for malignant melanoma was offered to possibly extend my life. Luckily, in spite of my age of 80, it was determined by Dr. Douglas Reintgen that I was a candidate for this surgery. "Some 60s are 80, but then some 80s are 60." He took me! This surgery was done at the Lakeland Cancer Center in Florida. The surgery nearly killed me, but it saved my life. Jack was also diagnosed with melanoma shortly after I was but not with the same outcome. His was not isolated.

Verma Boyd and Joanne started what became the Friday Group in 1973 to study Francis Schaeffer books. Joanne was a new congressional wife, and this fulfilled a need to stay focused on how we should live, fulfilling God's purpose for our lives. Dr. Schaeffer was thought of as the foremost evangelical thinker of our day. He had long pondered the fate of declining Western culture; he had concluded that not only have we lost sight of our roots but of our direction as well. However, unlike most doomsayers, he pinpointed the problems, researched their origins, and formulated a hopeful and positive proposal for the future.

As a member of the Friday Group, I was privileged to know the Schaeffers and their children and to study with Dr. Schaeffer and his wife, Edith. Jack and Joanne with the Friday Group sponsored Dr. Schaeffer's first meeting with members of Congress introducing his then new book *How Should We Then Live?* Their children continue to stay in touch, visiting with Joanne and the Friday Group when in the States.

Joanne encouraged a Bible study outside the Friday Group. Most attended Community Bible Study held at the First Presbyterian Church, Bethesda, Maryland, where Dr. Richard Halverson was pastor. Dr. Halverson became my pastor, my counselor, and friend. At one low point and needing his counsel, I went to the church and asked for him. He was in a meeting, but his staff had been told to notify him at any time for me. He came out and looked for the closest place for us to talk privately. It was the broom closet. You can only imagine the look on the face of the janitor when he opened the door to find me and Dr. Halverson. I called him when Sherri was to be married, and he only asked, "Where and when?" He was at that time chaplain of the senate.

The genesis of the Community Bible Study was through the efforts of Lee Campbell, another member of Joanne's Friday Group, and her husband, "Corky." In the beginning Anne Ruymann, Joanne's college roommate and Friday Group member, wrote the lessons for CBS. CBS has now grown worldwide. Patty Colson— then bride of Chuck Colson, Mary Godfrey— Arthur Godfrey's widow, and her daughter, Patty Godfrey Schmidt, were in my CBS small group.

Their love and support were with me during the trials. Anne wrote:

> You have been in my thoughts and prayers for many months and I want you to know how you have ministered to me through this long season of trials.

You have been loving, when it would have been so easy and so understandable to be unloving. Truly, your ability to so love has been God-given.

You have conveyed His Peace, Peace "which passes all understanding," although the circumstances were confusing and disrupting.

You have walked by faith, guided by the One who is "The Light of the World," in the midst of great darkness.

Your radiant countenance has reflected that "the joy of the Lord is your strength." (Neh.8:10)

The Lord has blessed me through you, Loraine. Thank you for being His servant and for allowing Him to live and shine through you.

I have mentioned Mary Glynn Peeples as an important person in my life. Even though I had been in the Church since Cradle Roll—my mother saw to that—it was Mary Glynn who led me to open the door and invite Jesus into my life for a personal relationship with him. It was then that I learned how a life could change when the Holy Spirit of God takes his rightful place in the heart of an individual. This most important decision certainly changed mine. From that day in 1975 when my world was falling apart, I knew that I could give all my cares and worries to him and he would take care of me. It is his promise, and I claimed it! From that day forward, I was never alone and have not been afraid.

Mary Glynn also impacted the lives of my children. On one very miserable late night in 1976 when I needed help, I called Mary Glynn and asked if she would please come over. She got out of bed, put on her robe, and without telling Sam, her husband, came to my home. She was help for me and also tried to comfort the children.

Twenty-five years after that night, John wrote Mary Glynn this letter:

> I feel this letter is long overdue. Up until recently, every time I heard your name, I would associate it with a very painful time for me and my family. I'm ashamed that you walked into my room that night and

found such an angry young boy amongst such a mess. I truly wish I had responded differently to you, but I think I was in a self preservation mode. I had learned not to let my guard down for fear of being terribly hurt. Unfortunately, this was also preventing the people who could have helped me from getting in. As a result, that was the beginning of a very rocky road of fights, suspension from school, and more.

But thank God, the story gets better. Mom probably has told you that this summer I broke my neck. In my free time, I decided to do something I've always wanted to do. I wanted to read the Bible. I started in the Old Testament but I found it hard to stay focused. I decided to move to the New Testament and found the jump-start that I needed. The good news is that I finished it and am now almost through Matthew on my second trip around. The unexpected news is that it sparked a curiosity that caused me to start investigating this whole God thing. Well, guess what? I am completely convinced that God is our Creator and that

His son, Jesus, lived and lives! But this then began to create a problem. If I were going to be completely convinced, that meant everything in the New Testament applied to me and it is true. This wasn't a Tom Clancy novel that I would put on the shelf or sell at the next garage sale once I was done with it. This was going to be the "Owner's Manual" for my life. What an incredible concept. This manual lays it all out: How we should live, how we should worship, how we should love. There is nothing left to question. Then I had to ask myself - how much am I going to let this whole God thing inconvenience my life as I have known it?

Well, it didn't take long to figure that one out. The Kingdom of God sounded much more appealing than the burning lake of fire.

So, this is where I am. I constantly pray for continued education and guidance. I realize that I need to do some housecleaning before I begin anything else, but I have committed myself to Him. This has been a life changing experience.

Some might say that a normal response would be "high fives" and celebration. My response has been internal turmoil. My poor wife, Kathy, thinks I'm possessed. I try to explain to her that this isn't something that I can try for a week or two and if it doesn't work, I'll return it for a full refund. It doesn't work that way. There is a God that sent his son to earth to assume all of my sins and was sacrificed for me. To do anything but sacrifice my life to Him would be the ultimate insult a man could make to his God. His Son will have died for nothing.

So, I've committed to the challenge. I've begun my walk with no intention of looking back. I keep the pain and persecution of my Christ Jesus and his apostles in my mind as my motivation. I write to you, Mary Glynn, in hopes of giving you renewed assurance that the Holy Spirit lives and is with us, and miracles are still happening even today.

God Bless you for being so faithful to Him for so many years. "Grace to all who love our Lord Jesus Christ with an undying love."

Others in Washington were hurting; I was not the only one. I invited wives of new members of Congress to a clandestine gathering in my home to hear Ann Kiemel and her twin sister, Jan Ream. Ann believed there was no such word as *impossible* in God's world. Her three books at the time were among the ten best sellers on the inspirational market. She was a much sought after speaker. Ann and Jan, herself a gifted communicator and psychologist, made a dynamic duo.

The women poured their hearts out to Ann and Jan, and lives were changed. Rosemary Trible from West Virginia later wrote a book giving me credit for wanting to help others at a time when I needed help the most. The book told her story shared with Ann and Jan that day in my home and gave them credit for life-changing advice.

Paul Miller, military liaison to the White House, was the man in charge of ceremonies for every president from Harry Truman to Ronald Reagan. That included inaugurations, official and state funerals, arrivals of heads of states, and commemorative ceremonies. Anytime the flag went by in the Military District of Washington, Paul was the one who set it waving. He dubbed me "my kissing cousin." My maiden name was Miller. His wife, Marie, and I worked on many projects together. I've mentioned the Christian Embassy. Marie and Paul even gave the rehearsal party for Sherri's wedding to Michael.

To my kissing Cousin Lorraine
Paul

The list is long of the people who have changed
the tapestry of my life, and I am a better person
for having known them.

14

MAKING MY OWN WAY

Faith is being sure of what we hope for and certain of what we do not see. (Hebrews 11:1)

Mrs. Robert Kennedy and I met at Hickory Hill, and we talked about how I could help. My friend had offered me "to put order in her life," and Mrs. Kennedy was persistent.

Anne Groer reported in the *Sentinel Star*:

> The woman who used to run the Republican household of Rep. Dick Kelly but who was dismissed in a divorce action now oversees one of the area's most prominent bastions of Democratic life—Ethel Kennedy's posh Virginia home, "Hickory Hill."
>
> The home has long been a social and political gathering place for the alumni of Jack Kennedy's Camelot.
>
> Loraine Kelly has been supervising the renovation of the four-floor, fifteen-bedroom home in the very affluent suburb of McLean, Va.

After our introductions and coffee served the morning we met, Mrs. Kennedy told me that she had just fired her decorator and needed help in decorating Hickory Hill for the senator's upcoming campaign. "Could I do it?" she asked.

This was about ten years after the death of her husband, Robert F. Kennedy, and she had not been coping well. Her world was falling apart. She was more of a Kennedy than most of the Kennedys and wanted to put her house in order to answer the call.

I asked Mrs. Kennedy after our meeting if I might take a look around the house and grounds before making a decision. It was obvious that she and this beautiful home needed help. Knowing that the Kennedys owned the Merchandise Mart in Chicago, this could be a piece of cake. I later learned that Mrs. Kennedy called my friend, Joanne Kemp, and asked if it were okay that she had hired me and how would she rate me in a scale of 1 to 10. Joanne told her more than 10. Now, that is a friend.

Working with the Merchandise Mart in Chicago and getting the commitment of Mr. Wray's workroom to stay with me until the project was completed made getting the design work done in record time. Success for me was best measured by Jackie Kennedy's reaction when she saw the changes for the first time. Mrs. Kennedy had asked me to greet guests as they arrived. Almost the first question asked by Jackie Kennedy was "Who did it?" Mrs. Kennedy gave the credit to me. The decorator fired by Ethel Kennedy was also at the first party and, after seeing the house, offered me a job.

Reports in the news, such as the dogs eating the food off the table before the guests had a chance at it, were better received by Mrs. Kennedy than an orderly house. She loved the chaos and was noted for it. She had a great sense of humor. She was famous for her valentines. The one I have is after losing Iowa in the election: Roses are red, cornflowers are blue, if you come from Iowa, phooey on you, Valentine! She was pictured on the valentine with a hog.

Senator Kennedy called ahead of one of the events and asked if I would see that the dogs were penned before his and Patrick's arrival. Patrick was highly allergic. I did as he asked until Mrs. Kennedy missed the dogs. That was that. The senator and Patrick left early.

The work getting the house in order was completed about midnight before the day of the first event. Mrs. Kennedy had asked earlier to take a walk with her to look around the house and grounds. She even looked over the fence enclosing the dumpster and commented that she had never seen a place so clean and in such good order. She was very pleased with the work that had been done.

Four of the eleven children were still at home when I undertook the job: Christopher (Chris), Maxwell (Max), Douglas (Doug) and Rory. Rory was born after her father's death but in the same year. I felt much like a surrogate mother to them and mentored some of the older ones.

Mary Courtney Kennedy married Jeff Ruhe June 14, 1980. Jeff was a TV producer in New York and was such a nice guy. I remember Mrs. Kennedy buying Courtney a television because she thought that would keep Courtney at her place in New York and not spend so much time at Jeff's. The reception at Hickory Hill was covered by *People Magazine*. So typical of the Kennedys, even before wedding pictures were taken at Hickory Hill, Courtney was pushed into the pool by her brothers. The wet wedding dress still on her was dried with hair dryers, and the party continued.

Even though their vows to each other were to "be true to you in good times and in bad, in sickness and in health, I will love you and honor you and be one with you now and forever," they divorced in 1990. Courtney remarried in 1993 to human rights activist Paul Hill.

The senator's fundraiser was on July 26, 1980. Mrs. Kennedy was at the Cape during this event but several of the older children attended.

The Cellar Door produced the concert. The performers were Mary Wells of Peter, Paul and Mary, the Drifters, the Coasters, Gary, and the U.S. Band. The rock bands were staged near the cabana and pool. My political experience with Kelly's campaigns came in handy. The Secret Service was very protective and did a great job. Thousands came; the event was a huge success. In fact, getting the guests to leave became a big problem.

About midnight I called the police, not to make any arrests but to help clear the grounds. They were asked to come to the front of the house without lights and sirens. But of course they came with all the fanfare they could muster, and people scattered everywhere. I did not know that Bobby was still outside. He made the quickest dash from the garden to the top floor of the house to open a window and shout down, "Officers, is there a problem?" Asleep on the second floor was Rebecca, Bobby's girlfriend at the time, who was a house guest.

My son, John, caused a bit of a problem. The rock band members thought him to be a Kennedy and gave him special attention and shared their "refreshments." He was out of control and was having too much fun. I asked the Secret Service to take him to the sauna, but in no time, I saw his blonde head streaking through the crowd again.

Another special event was the engagement party for Vickie and Michael.

> Maxine and Frank Gifford take great pleasure in announcing the engagement of their daughter, Victoria Denise, to Michael LeMoyne Kennedy, son of Mrs. Robert F. Kennedy and the late Senator Kennedy. Victoria and Michael plan a March (1981) wedding at St. Ignatius Loyola Church in New York City.

Bobby's engagement to Emily Black was initially not celebrated. Bobby called from the University of Virginia where both were students and asked to speak with his mother about getting married. Mrs. Kennedy hung up on him; the call did not go well. Maybe this was too much of a surprise. He called back to ask if I would stand in for his mother at his wedding to Emily. I suggested that he give his mother a little time and talk with her again. Bobby and Emily were married in April 1982.

Kerry Kennedy attended Brown University and would bring her roommate, Mary Richardson, home with her during school breaks. Bobby divorced Emily in 1992 and married Mary in 1994.

Hickory Hill was a busy house while I was there in 1979–1981. The happiest sounds in the house were during Andy Williams's stay. The house was filled with music. He was appearing at the Kennedy Center and stayed at Hickory Hill. Ethel Kennedy attended the concert as his guest. It was rumored and published that he was dating Ethel Kennedy, but it was not true. The two families were very good friends. It was too important to her to remain a Kennedy.

Mrs. Kennedy wanted me to go with her to the Cape for the summers, but I could not unless I could take the children. John was with me, and Sherri would be coming home from Vanderbilt for the summer. We agreed on hiring a person for the Cape, and I would stay at Hickory Hill.

Getting the family packed for their routine holiday trips was always a monumental undertaking. The travel was mostly done in the Skakel's private plane.

Alexa Halaby, Queen Noor's sister, stayed with us at Hickory Hill the summer before leaving for law school in Texas. Joe visited during that summer and invited Sherri to party with them. Alexa was protective of Sherri and vetoed the invitation.

There was also another Bobby visit while Sherri was home that summer. Sherri and I shared a bedroom on the fourth floor. I knew to lock the door that evening and even pushed my bed against it. His behavior seemed suspicious. In the middle of the night, as expected, Bobby was banging on the door. When he arrived in a taxi that evening from the airport with his dog, he paid the fare and slammed the car door on his dog's tail. The dog then crashed through the front screen door swishing his stubby tail and spattering blood on everything in its path. The house was museum like and the cleanup was enormous. The next morning's news reported his arrival in DC and his being briefly detained before arriving at Hickory Hill.

David had traveled to California with his parents and was in his hotel room upstairs watching television when he witnessed his father's assassination in the kitchen below. He was thirteen at the time. David died in 1984 of drug overdose at age twenty-nine. He was the person you would want to take home with you.

Routinely, the family would go to Cape Cod for the summers, to Vermont skiing at Thanksgiving, and to Aspen or Vail for Christmas. Christmas was an early gathering of all the family before leaving for Colorado. Shopping, gift wrapping, and organizing the gift stations in the drawing room for every member of the family was huge.

Courtney wrote in February 1980:

I just want you to know how much I appreciated your help during the last few months. Christmas has always been a hectic time, but you made everything go so smoothly even with the added complications of an engagement party, a fund-raiser, a christening, etc.

I think that you are the greatest asset to our home since Ena, and I hope that you will be there for quite a while (as difficult as it sometimes is).

Ena was the black woman who had reared all of the children at Hickory Hill. This was putting me in good company. Mrs. Kennedy's note read, "You are a wonder."

I took on much more than redecorating the house and getting the house in order. There were piles of unanswered mail and rumors of unpaid bills. There was work to be done on the Robert F. Kennedy Memorial, the RFK Foundation, the Hickory Hill Pet Show, and later, even taking on the finances of Hickory Hill.

Mrs. Kennedy always gave me challenges, testing me. This became a game shared with her friends. The date in May was set for the annual pet show at Hickory Hill to benefit Runaway House, a counseling and foster care program for young people. Art Buchwald was to be the ringmaster, and she wanted Barbara Woodhouse, the famous British dog trainer, as the star of the show. She asked me to take care of it. Mrs. Woodhouse accepted Mrs. Kennedy's invitation but requested tickets on the Concorde for herself and her husband delivered to her home within the week. Each ticket cost $7,000. Where was this money coming from? I called Steve Smith in the New York office and explained my dilemma. He gave me credit card information to fund the tickets with my promise that it would be paid back within the month. What was I thinking? And what was he thinking about me? The two tickets were delivered, and the show did go on and was a huge success.

Maybe this bold move encouraged Steve Smith to invite me to the next Ethel Kennedy financial meeting in New York. I told him that I needed Mrs. Kennedy's approval to attend. He took care of that. I did attend the meeting, and Steve Smith asked if I would stay over, again asking for Mrs. Kennedy's approval. Rose Kennedy had a Park Avenue apartment overlooking Central Park, and it was made available to me. This was looking good. If I'm to stay, I asked if it would be possible for me to get a ticket to *Evita* then playing on Broadway. The Kennedys just happened to have a box. I got settled in and went down for the doorman's assistance in getting a ride to the show. He was hailing a taxi when I asked if it could be a horse-drawn carriage. Imagine my riding down Park Avenue to the theatre all by myself in a horse-drawn carriage. Seated directly in front of me at the theatre were George Burns and Gracie Allen. Look what was possible just for the asking.

The next morning I reported for work in the New York office of the Kennedy dynasty. Steve Smith, husband of Jean Kennedy and manager of all Kennedys, expressed his pleasure in having good help in managing Hickory Hill and the Ethel Kennedy family. This much sought after job had been held before by young women just out of college who were eager to be close to the

Kennedys but who possessed little or none of the necessary experience needed. For three days, I was given all the past records needed to set a new budget for Mrs. Kennedy. Imagine my telling Mrs. Kennedy how to spend her money. Nevertheless, the new budget was set. I told Steve Smith that he was setting me up for trouble.

Kathleen and I were in Rose Kennedy's New York apartment together for a night during the financial meeting. She was in New York to make a television appearance for her mother. This was an opportunity to mention to her my plan to phase out the older children's contribution to their mother's budget over a three-year period. She could not have been more pleased. I'm sure that this was an item overlooked as the children got older and left home.

Kathleen Kennedy was the oldest of Ethel and Robert Kennedy's children, and I think she was the most well-adjusted. Having had more time with her father could have made the difference. She was born in 1951, and her father was killed June 6, 1968, at age forty-two. She married David Lee Townsend, a professor, in 1973, and she later served as lieutenant governor of Maryland.

Mrs. Kennedy came from wealth equal to the Kennedys'. She was accustomed to shopping and having someone else taking care of the payment. She would expect the clerk to know who she was and treat her accordingly, delivering the purchase to Hickory Hill along with the bill for payment. Maybe this is a bygone way of doing business, but it appeals to me. The reported bad reputation for payment came from inexperienced help not knowing how to process the bills. I even had to promise Mr. Whay whose workroom I used in decorating Hickory Hill that he would be paid on time and in full.

When I was leaving Hickory Hill, I called Steve Smith in New York to tell him that I felt I was letting him down by leaving before getting the spending under control. His response was "Robert Kennedy couldn't do it. How could he expect it of me?" Spending, understandably, was more during my time at Hickory Hill because of the campaign.

A very happy memory of Hickory Hill was the summer I invited my bridge group from Zephyrhills, Florida, to visit. We had the entire house to ourselves, and they later prepared a photo album of the trip for me.

Another was the week I took off to meet friends, Joan Randall and her two children, at the Cape; we were taking the ferry to Nantucket. She and the children had taken a road trip to Connecticut, and I was to join them for a stay at the White Elephant. When my plane arrived, Joan told me that I was being paged, much to my surprise. Mrs. Kennedy was told about this trip but did not know my plans. She had sent a driver to have us come to the Kennedy Compound to have lunch and invited us to stay. What a treat! I still remember arriving at her home and seeing white, lace-trimmed pantaloons on the clothesline swaying in the breeze. This had to have been staged. It was too perfect a picture.

I think Ethel Kennedy allowed me to get closer to her than few others had. She would, from time to time, ask me to pray for her. I could have remained at Hickory Hill as she asked, but my children would have taken back seats, and I would not have had a life. I would have been living hers.

I rejected a book deal to write about the least known of the Kennedy women.

Tampa Tribune, June 2, 1986:

> Loraine Kelly still is reserved in what she'll say, for print or otherwise, about the Kennedys. There are a lot of reasons for her caution— among them, not wanting to damage the family or unwittingly compromise their security.
>
> She also has an apparent distaste for saying anything unflattering about anyone. But Loraine Kelly, who apparently believes that moral obligations come with privileged knowledge, had kept the faith.

The Kennedy experience has been noted with affection.

Newspapers reported that I was exploring, going from "Hill to Hill: Hickory Hill to Capitol Hill."

After leaving Hickory Hill, I did go to Florida to determine if I had the support and could raise the necessary funds to make a successful bid to represent my home district in Congress. I could do this for someone else; could I do it for myself?

What was the largest district had now been divided, and my home district was comparatively small; therefore, I felt I could win this one sitting on the front porch. The reception and support were overwhelming.

"Considered at least as politically savvy as her husband" was reported. Friends were encouraging me to run for Congress.

My car was still packed. I had just returned from two months in Florida, and the phone rang. The caller identified herself as Marilyn Widney from New York, wanting to know if I knew Ana and Juan. They had worked for me at Hickory Hill, but most of the help left after I did. She asked if I knew Prospect House in Georgetown and if I would consider meeting with her. I thought I was going to help Ana and Juan. They had registered with an employment agency to find a job. Marilyn Widney had called that agency to get help in protecting the property just purchased until plans could be made to restore and decorate one of the "*Great Houses of Washington, D.C.*" (Hope Ridings Miller).

Prospect House was a private Georgetown residence built in 1788. It was used by the government of the United States as an official guest house while President and Mrs. Harry Truman lived at Blair House during a major renovation of the White House.

The meeting went well for me but not for Ana and Juan. The keys to Prospect House were put in my hand. The job was mine if I wanted it. At that time, I didn't even know what the job would be. It was then that I explained that I could not take on this responsibility until I had made a decision about running for Congress. This only intrigued Marilyn Widney more. I was told, if I would protect her investment, I could take as much time as was needed to make that decision but with the understanding that everything possible would be done to keep me with her. She then got in her limousine and went back to New York.

> The news that Loraine Kelly . . . is thinking about running for Congress next year changes the whole complexion of that race. Ms. Kelly has many friends in that district and has long been looked on as a well-informed, highly intelligent lady with plenty of political appeal . . . In Pinellas County Ms. Kelly has already started to pick

up impressive GOP support . . . With this effort snowballing, many say Ms. Kelly could be a serious contender *if* she decides to make the race. In other words, don't sell her short by any means. (*Pinellas Review,* October 2, 1981)

The Republican National Committee offered a training program for congressional candidates in Washington. I enrolled, thinking that I should keep putting myself to the test until a decision was made.

I lobbied as many of the Florida delegation as possible as a courtesy and wanting their reaction to my candidacy. These visits were encouraging.

One evening as I was leaving Senator Paula Hawkins's office, I met Bill Armstrong, senator from Colorado and husband of Ellen, in the hall. He asked what I was doing. When told, he said, "Go and I will help you." Jack Kemp pledged the same. With this kind of help and with so many Florida friends encouraging me to go for it, the quest continued.

Most of my adult life had been in politics and therefore was very public. The children did not want me to run believing that Congress had been the downfall of our family.

As the days passed doing double duty with the work at Prospect House and continuing the pursuit of a decision of whether to run for Congress or not, I was really enjoying the time out and the time off the merry-go-round of politics. For the first time in my adult life I was out of reach of the press. God was opening another door. Prospect House became a safe haven, and I was very comfortable doing what I loved to do. At Hickory Hill and now Prospect House, my domestic side had found outlets.

When all things were considered and a decision made to stay with Prospect House, this letter, in part, was sent to friends and supporters:

> Thank you for your warm reception and encouragement while considering a run for Congress to represent our district. Your response was overwhelming.

For more than twenty years we have worked and played together and have shared good times and bad. We have fought the good fights and are stronger for them. Your support of me and my family has been heartwarming. But most of all, I thank you for giving us such tremendous opportunities for growth and service at home and in Washington. For this, I will be eternally grateful.

My decision not to run at this time is based on family responsibilities and professional considerations. I am sure you will understand.

My first assignment at Prospect House was to find the top designers in the country who specialized in decorating period homes. Four design firms were chosen from different parts of the country and sent to New York for Mrs. Widney to make the final decision. The H. Chambers Company based in Baltimore, Maryland, was chosen to do the decoration.

The former owners of Prospect House had taken all of the very old and beautiful chandeliers out of the house and had replaced them with poor substitutes. The originals had to be recovered and reinstalled. This was the beginning of the restoration of this historic property.

Within a few days it was determined that a more practical arrangement would be for me to move into Prospect House. A friend later remarked that God had certainly given me two beautiful places to live, without my even asking: Hickory Hill and now, Prospect House.

My home in McLean had been sold as required in the divorce, and John had returned from Florida and was now in McLean High School. I had moved to a rental townhouse and had taken in renters to help with expenses. My first renter was Homa Taylor, who was Iranian. She had married a U.S. naval officer she believed to have been murdered. She fled Iran and had lost everything during the overthrow of the Shah. She became a very good friend.

The H. Chambers Company team had come to take measurements and photos in preparation for their presentation of the work they proposed to do. With this team was my introduction to Steve O'Brien, who became one of my Washington children. He was from Alabama and quickly attached to me from Georgia. He was spending so much time with me that his mother came to check me out. This also happened with Babs, a sorority sister of Sherri's at Vanderbilt. Sherri had told Babs when she accepted a job in Washington to contact me for any help needed in setting up her apartment. Babs's mother wanted to know my intentions. I told her that I hoped she would have done the same for Sherri if she had located in Cincinnati and needed help. They thought me strange.

Prospect House was built in 1788 in the Federal style by General James McCubbin Lingan, a colorful revolutionary war hero, prominent merchant, and distinguished member of local society. As with many Washingtonians, politics was his undoing. A staunch Federalist, he published an editorial denouncing President Madison's war policies and was consequently stoned to death by an angry mob.

But long before Lingan met his bloody fate, he had sold the grand house on the bluff above the river. Prospect House is not a family homestead; indeed, it has been used for far-from-family purposes. During the Truman administration, when Blair House served as the presidential residence, it became the official guesthouse for visiting potentates. Mary Steele Morris, whose family occupied the house for several generations, held séances there, and it is said that she regularly invoked the shades of the past.

As befits a great house with access to the Potomac, several of its occupants have been associated with the navy. One owner was William Marbury, a naval agent who bought the house in 1801. When James V. Forrestal, secretary of the navy, acquired it in 1945, he often commuted to work by motorboat. After Forrestal's death, his widow sold the house to their friend Thurman Chatham, a North Carolina manufacturer and naval man who subsequently became a congressman. (Forrestal jumped from the tower of the Bethesda Naval Hospital. A friend across the street told me of evenings sitting on the front steps visiting with Forrestal, who was a very sensitive man. He felt that the load had just gotten too heavy for Forrestal to carry.)

If Prospect House were built by a war hero, its gardens were propagated by a southern gentleman, a man as passionate about peace as General Lingan was about war. A man who vowed that he would do nothing in half measures, Thurman Chatham came to Washington with many passions: peace, flowers, the sea, polo, flying, and politics. He brought with him not only a wife who shared his enthusiasms for gardening and politics but also boxwoods he had rooted at his farm near Elkin, North Carolina. With the help of Mina Bruce Haldeman, a landscape architect from Glenview, Kentucky, the Chathams proceeded to create a garden on the steep bank of the Potomac.

The garden at Prospect House was an old established garden when I arrived, and it was essentially as the Chathams designed it but had long been neglected. The garden is terraced, creating garden rooms. Closest to Prospect Street and highest in elevation is a naturalized garden dominated by a magnificent elm, under which, it was said then, had stood every American president since Washington. Rosy brick steps lead down to the formal garden. The view of the Potomac from the end of the formal garden was a great spot for afternoon tea. A few more steps down lead to a swimming pool amid abundantly producing pear trees and peonies.

Perhaps the best view of the Potomac is from the gazebo. Connected by a catwalk to the dining room, the two-story tower with its pyramidal roof looks to the modern eye to be purely ornamental. It originally allowed the merchants who owned

Prospect House to watch for their ships. Evidence discovered in the 1930s indicates that at least one resident had augmented his fortune by trading slaves; a tunnel runs between the gazebo and the river, and on its walls are heavy iron rings.

From the gazebo, walk through a gate to a rose garden which was added during my time. The rose garden was on the foundation of an old tobacco warehouse.

This information was shared with Bettz Burr from Asheville, North Carolina, and published in the May–June 1989 issue of *Southern Accents*, "Hospitality on the Potomac: The Convivial Formal Garden of Georgetown's Prospect House." She invited me to the Biltmore. She was intrigued by the work I was doing; I even thought she was interested in my job.

> When asked about her qualifications for her job, Kelly laughs and says, "I do windows." The self-effacing answer is far from literal. Kelly manages a large staff and has an army of professionals on call. But her reply symbolized the spirit in which she approaches her work. It is the spirit of Vesta,

goddess of the hearth and home, perhaps the most honored yet least known of all the Roman deities. Imbued with the history of the house, Kelly makes sure that preserves and tarts are made from the crop of pears down by the pool, that flowers are cut to fill the vases, and that the aroma of freshly baked bread greets visitors. She is there to manage, but primarily she sees that the house and garden are enjoyed in all their seasons.

In her role as caretaker-curator, she provides the continuity and cosseting every historical house needs.

In the meantime, while plans were being made for decorating the house, the gardens were being restored to their "original magnificence." The gardens of Prospect House were then chosen to be in the archives of Garden Clubs of America in New York as one of the most beautiful gardens in America.

In due course, the Chambers representatives came to Prospect House and made a presentation of their design to Mrs. Widney and me. When I saw the cost of doing the small garden apartment that could be my living quarters, I suggested allowing me to furnish this part to meet my needs and to satisfy future use of the space, at half the cost. Who could refuse that offer?

The apartment was furnished in record time and within the half-price budget. As a result, decorating the entire house became my project. Mrs. Widney knew that she had the help she needed and could cut out the middle man.

Learning more about decorating a period home would be to my advantage. The Smithsonian had classes in almost any interest imaginable. I needed to know what liberties could be taken in making the furniture comfortable and making the furnishings family friendly while staying true to the Federal period. Night classes were taken at the Smithsonian, and the curator of Tudor Place was also most helpful. The owner benefited also by my having a designer's license to practice in DC, Virginia, and Maryland.

Washington had every resource needed to bring this beautiful historic home back to its glory days. The team helping me was the best.

Two of my congressional-wife friends had formed an events business and approached me about using the house for special events. The owners were agreeable, if I were willing to take this own. World Bank would take over Washington for a week and would use Prospect House. Mobil Oil often used the house for their board meetings. They were among many to enjoy and appreciate Prospect House. The house was even used in the filming of *Deep Impact*. Booking such events, mostly on my time and long hours, more than paid my salary.

Georgetown University was across the street from Prospect House. The dorms were shown as the hospital in the movie *The Exorcist*. Most scenes were filmed in the house on the other side of the Car Barn attached to Prospect House. The very steep steps in the movie, where the head was shown rolling, were attached to the Car Barn but were shown to be attached to the house. Some scenes were filmed in Prospect House. Peter Blatty, author of *The Exorcist*, lived in the next block on Prospect Street.

What I thought would be a short-term undertaking became twenty-three years. It seemed that my make-sense suggestions kept making the job grow.

Initially, I was led to believe that Mrs. Widney had purchased the house. And at that time, it was believed that elite Georgetown would not tolerate Arabs invading their domain.

Georgetown residents live behind high walls, closed doors, and garden fences. They slide their cars into narrow slots and dart in and out of their houses almost furtively. Their neighborhood is not their own. The sidewalks and streets belong to the students with backpacks, jeans, and slouchy jackets; on weekends, the two commercial avenues—M and Wisconsin—are thronged with tourists drawn by chic shops and trendy restaurants. In such a setting, one's home is a well-guarded castle; one's garden, a private paradise.

My neighbors in Georgetown over time were Senator Pell diagonally across the street, Jonda and Bud McFarlane in the next block, John Kerry and Teresa Heinz, Sally and Ben Bradley, LaBelle and Bert Lance, to name a few. LaBelle Lance lived across the street from my friend Dorie

Sills, who was introduced to me by Mary Glynn. LaBelle Lance was in our Bible study with Mary Glynn; sometimes, meeting in her home.

When I eventually met the real owner of Prospect House who was from the United Arab Emirates, and he then met Sherri, he asked if I would do for his girls what I had done for her. He had six. They were to be placed in American universities, and I was to be their surrogate mother. I soon learned that damage control was most needed. Mrs. Widney had been placing in colleges the first of the girls to come to the U.S., but she assigned me all the tasks involved in getting them settled. The first purchase for each student was any car of their choice. When the veil is taken off, look out world. One of the girls even gave a birthday party for herself and invited the entire college.

I became Marilyn Widney's valued helper. Special requests were as varied as entrée to DC events, the Design Center, and people of interest to her; they range from obtaining tapes of all John Kennedy's speeches, to getting an electric gate and chicken wire for a farm in England, or to decorating a house in Dubai. She would require my help with personal parties given at her place in New York. I was one of the first called for help when hurricane Hugo damaged her home in Charleston. The more she leaned on me, the more intimidated/threatened she became.

The New York office of the corporation covering Prospect House headed by Marilyn Widney was eventually closed and moved to Washington. She was relieved of her duties when incriminating information against her was revealed by discrepancies in her records not agreeing with mine being reported to Dubai.

When more of the girls came for college at American University, I suggested, rather than renting quarters for them, why not have them live with me in Prospect House. This was a good move for the girls, but it did make the business of the house more challenging. Their privileged background left little tolerance for their being second to any business of the house, and there was even less consideration for my personal space and time.

When the one son came to Washington, a lavish apartment was furnished for him near American University. The biggest and best for the son—that was the custom. He could not be housed with the girls. The son was lovable and was a playboy. He stayed for four years with few or no transferable credits. This is how buildings got named. He later attended college in London. How pleased I would be if he were to appear at my front door.

Over time with the family, there were babies born, graduations, weddings, homes furnished, much shopping and shipping, teaching the children to paint, and much more. And then, children of those children began arriving.

I had just told the owner's wife on one of her visits that I was thinking about retiring and doing for my children and grandchildren what I was doing for hers. Her response was "I thought you would always be with us."

It was then that moisture was causing wallpaper to buckle on the lower level. Every possible cause was explored, and repairs were made as needed, but the problems continued. It was eventually determined that the old iron steam pipes from the furnace, probably about eighty years old, had been deteriorating over time until steam from the pipes finally found an outlet through the beautiful wooden floors. Boards had to be removed until the source of the problem was found. A three-foot deep ditch was dug, following the bad pipe extending the length of the lower level, until good pipe that could be threaded was found. This was a mammoth undertaking and was made urgent by scheduled events, one of which was being hosted by the owner from Dubai.

The insurance adjuster was called to assess the damage, and help was called to get the repairs started as quickly as possible. The good work relationship established over the years with excellent helpers/superior craftsmen paid off. Ronnie and Joe should be named as the first responders.

When the wallpaper was removed in my office, one could have planted a garden. My living quarters in the garden apartment, which included my office, were on the lower level of the house with the furnace room. For several years I had been going to every doctor I could find—and any suggested by others—to find a cause for my fainting, but it was to no avail. The adjuster called the specialists to remove the black mold, and when he suggested that I see a doctor as soon as possible, I knew I was in trouble. He told of his most recent case of a woman who had been living with the mold for about three years and had died. We guessed that it had taken about ten years for the pipes to disintegrate and for this problem to manifest itself.

Luckily one of the doctors that I had seen had just returned from an American Medical Association meeting. The main speaker's topic was on black mold, which few doctors at the time knew anything about. She suggested that I see this doctor as soon as possible and hoped that I would be willing to go to Ohio. There was some urgency in her voice.

I flew to Ohio and was tested by Dr. Boyles in Centerville. Black mold was determined to be my problem. For two years I had weekly shots of serum in each hip supplied by this doctor and took about a dozen pills each day to restore my destroyed immune system. This imposed an extra burden during an already difficult time.

The doctor advised that if I wanted to live, I should vacate Prospect House immediately. I thought of the repairs needed for the upcoming scheduled events, one being for the owner.

When I asked for reimbursement of the medical expenses incurred because of the black mold, the owner referred me to his New York lawyer, as was the custom. The lawyer did not want to acknowledge that black mold in the house was my health problem even though it was the insurance adjuster telling me to get help. It should have been no surprise that I was told by him to get myself a lawyer. I had been told this by him before on another occasion. I could see a court case coming on.

The owner not returning my calls to ask if he approved of the advice I received from his lawyer was puzzling. He and I had always had a very good work relationship and communicated directly. I could be in touch with him at any time. I questioned where this Harvard-educated lawyer, who was being paid to protect him, was taking this. This was not what I wanted, and I'm sure it would not have been what the owner would have wanted. A front page story in the *Washington Post* at the time about a black mold case suing for millions may have caused him to think about his being a part of something big. I was only asking for expenses. This is the path Marilyn Widney would have chosen.

Through congressional friends, I found a lawyer asking just for my expenses. Wanting to know more about Prospect House, we agreed to meet at the house to talk about my case. He arrived in a Lamborghini with a car tag "ISUE4U." I cringed, but he was the New York lawyer's match. I was most uncomfortable during this meeting because a host family member was in the house.

In preparing the case, the owner's lawyer went to the expense of confiscating every file from Prospect House, taking them to New York to examine, surely thinking he would find incriminating evidence against me. I was comfortable in knowing that there was nothing in the files that had not been copied to New York and Dubai. The information in the files had to be shared with my lawyer. In doing so, the owner's lawyer caused a blunder of his own to expose personal information about the family. He would have also learned in examining the files that Marilyn Widney had purged her files before they were delivered to Prospect House.

Not a surprise when the case was over, the owner's lawyer required my signing a waiver of any future health claims and an agreement that I would forever have no contact with any member of a family I had been a part of for twenty-three years, even being a surrogate mother to the children. He had to be concerned about my exposing him.

The owner will never know the monumental effort, determination, and dedication involved in getting the restoration completed for his benefit under the most difficult circumstances made even worse by his lawyer.

My health concerns were put on hold to my detriment until the restoration was completed. I should have left without restoring the house. It would have been impossible for them to have gotten the house ready in time for his event and the other scheduled ones. The lawyer's representative from Baltimore was reporting that he could do the repairs while undermining me but obviously wanting me to get the job done, even telling me that it would be better if I did the restoration. He knew my sources for help would not be available to him, and he had no local help.

He and the lawyer would then have experienced the work involved, and the scheduled events would have been cancelled or rescheduled, if help were available. This Baltimore representative was puzzled by my being so calm during the chaos.

They knew nothing of the long hours involved in maintaining an historic property and taking on specials events. Only Marilyn Widney realized the benefits that came with my being an interior designer and having come to Prospect House with established contractors on call. Their lawyer told me at the end that he didn't have a clue what I did; yet he had chosen the person indirectly to replace me when I left. Replace me at doing what? The owner had asked if I would train the person taking over, were I to leave. I had agreed.

Marilyn Widney did not come by her role representing families in the Arab world by accident. Charles Widney, her short-term husband, was her introduction. He and his family were from Charleston, South Carolina, and had a grand antebellum home on Broad Street. Charles had business associates and good friends in the Middle East. Her story recounting the marriage and his death left questions unanswered. His death gave Marilyn the opportunity she wanted to take his place. What she lacked in ability, she ruled by brawn, noise, and brute force. She was on payroll as the widow of Charles until her death.

The last conversation I had with Marilyn was about wanting me to come live with her, promising half of everything she owned if I would. I could not.

Everyone has the cancer gene. It is my belief that my cancer was allowed to attack because of the black mold having destroyed my immune system. "Melanoma is unique because we have experience that it reacts with the immune system" (Dr. James Huth, a UT Southwestern surgical oncologist). The cause of spasmodic dysphonia is unknown; that disorder manifested itself at the same time.

Prospect House was restored. The owner and his New York lawyer enjoyed a beautiful evening made possible by me. I left knowing that I had fulfilled my responsibilities and could be at peace about a job completed and well done. It was a proud house again, ready for family and events. Someday the family will learn that I remained loyal to them, and their family remained private with me. I appreciated the close relationship I had with every family member involved and their courtesy and respect toward me in every instance, except at the end. I left knowing that I had given them more than they had given me.

Dr. Halverson had said, "You go nowhere by accident. Wherever you go, God is sending you. Wherever you are, God has put you there."

Mine is not to reason why.

15

RETIREMENT

For every door that closes

The time had come for me to leave Washington and be with family. I had always known that God would let me know when the time was right. John's response to my leaving was that I needed a swift kick to get the message.

Black mold gave me that kick. The house was cured, but my healing could not begin until I vacated the house.

On December 2004, after thirty years in Washington, I returned home on St. Simons Island. John was keeping Sherri's children while she was visiting her dad. He had bought a one-way ticket for me to return with him to Idaho. He and Kathy had been putting an addition on their home for two years, and indecision was killing them.

When Sherri returned, John and I left for Idaho to complete the project; in six weeks the house was done. This was not an easy project but was completed in record time, even though I had a bad fall which injured my left arm and right ankle. Work continued on the project even though trips to the hospital were necessary for treatment of my injuries. I had never seen gangrene before and was lucky I did not lose my arm.

A friend of John's, Suzanne, also a real estate agent, took me for an outing just before I was to leave for home. John's motive, as it had been for some time in putting us together, was for me to find a house in Idaho for the summers. John wanted his family closer. After a nice lunch, she asked what location would be my choice if I were to buy a house in Coeur d'Alene. We looked in the Fort Grounds area and then my second choice, Sanders Beach. We took a drive along the lake front and saw much in between the beach and the park, but still there was nothing for me.

Just as we were leaving and approaching McEuen Park and City Hall, to the right I saw a little blue Victorian house that was positioned exactly as I would want within walking distance of everything. But it was not for sale. Luckily, Suzanne knew the owners and the history of the house that might make it available if a reasonable offer were made. The Victorian style was my least favorite, but location trumped everything. Taking a leap of faith, an offer was made on Monday, and the closing was on Friday before my leaving to go back to the Island to heal.

When I returned to the Island, my schedule was just as busy as ever, even with the injuries. So I decided to return to Idaho and check out what I had bought. The house became a family project that summer of 2005, and a lot of sweat equity was involved.

A dream had come true, to have a gathering place for the family near John. Nothing ever works exactly as we dream; but we keep on dreaming, hoping, and praying, knowing that with God's help, anything is possible. Even so, we have shared some good times with family and friends but most of all enjoying every opportunity to be with grandchildren. Coeur d'Alene has it all, with the beautiful lake, mountains, and resort. My hope is that someone in the family will take charge and continue this family tradition after I am gone.

The summer of 2009 came closest to fulfilling my purpose for having the Coeur d'Alene house. More family members came to be with me, John, and his family than any other summer. Getting us a Lund fishing boat added great pleasure to our fishing and extended our activities on the beautiful lakes in the area. Open house during the summer months brought great joy sharing with family and friends. Will, my brother, came for the first time, and we celebrated his birthday.

My sister-in-law prepared a photo book as a thank you for their visit and included the following:

> This book contains pictures of a visit to Coeur d'Alene, Idaho, to celebrate the 80th birthday of Will Miller. A family visit filled with places we went, food we ate, and exciting things we shared. Family memories that will last for many years are recorded in the pages of this book.

I especially loved the last page:

God made us a family! We need one another, we love one another, we forgive one another, we work together, we play together, we pray together, we grow together!

Our family is a circle of strength and love. With every birth and every union, the circle grows. Every joy shared adds more love. Every crisis faced together makes the circle stronger!

Returning to St. Simons Island was coming home, and I was enjoying being with family and connecting with old friends. Sherri and her four children had been back from England for five years. I had never lived in the same location with either of my children. Being with John and his family in Idaho during the summer months and with Sherri and her family on the Island was more than I could have ever dreamed.

My first stop when I returned to the Island was the St. Simons Community Church, and I talked with Laura at the receptionist's desk. I told her that I had just moved back home and had left the National Presbyterian Church and a Friday Group Bible study family that I had been a part of since 1975. They knew me well. I told Laura that coming to SSCC was self-serving. Being in the last quarter of my life and starting over establishing a church home and family was a foremost concern. I needed and wanted to be a part of a church family here and for them to know me. Family members including grandchildren were already at SSCC; therefore, I did not consider any other church. Also, it still warms my heart to hear Larry Wade and Bev, Joe Fendig and others along with Kim, who is my niece, and her husband, Tom, greeting me as "Aunt Rene." We were family. I had known some of the parents of these young people, who had included Sherri from time to time in their activities.

It took about two years to find my place again in a community I called home. Much had changed in the more than fifty years of my being away and was compounded by the deaths of my mother and sister who lived on East Beach. The void was filled when I was claimed by a Home Group much like my Friday Group in Washington. God promises that he will fill our every need. Steve Temmer, an associate pastor of SSCC, asked the Reeves and the Ashes to take me in. Then, I had the church family on the Island and the support that again was so soon needed to survive a fight for my life.

Sherri and Mitchell gave me a big eightieth birthday party like no other at their home on Wildlife Drive and was a measure of what God can do. Over a hundred friends came to celebrate with me. My birthday was also celebrated by my Friday Group in Washington and the Gates community. How blessed I was.

I had signed on for a St. Simons Community Church mission trip and had gone to Mayo in Jacksonville for a three-day physical to get a clear bill of health before going to China. I had outlived my doctor in Washington and had not had a physical in ten years. It was there that I learned I had a malignant melanoma on my right leg. Treatment began for this one and several to follow until Mayo told me that they could do no more. Almost as an afterthought, I was given three choices of locations for a special treatment but with no promises. A radical surgery, a hyperthermic isolated limb perfusion for malignant melanoma, by Dr. Douglas Reintgen in November 2008 at the Lakeland Regional

Cancer Center, Lakeland, Florida, helped in saving my life. A heart attack during surgery extended my stay at the hospital. After returning home, everything that could go wrong after surgery did. I was in and out of the local hospital until January. Mitchell (Sherri's husband) and Marsha (Mitchell's sister) were my local doctors and were instrumental in getting every medical need met. My going back to Lakeland was out of the question. My SSCC Home Group became my support system and worked with Sherri in caring for my every other need. We really bonded as family.

God does amazing work. I later learned from Mary Glynn that her brother had a part in pioneering this treatment.

16

OVERVIEW OF EVENTS AND TRAVEL

You go nowhere by accident

This overview of my life as the wife of Richard Kelly and about survival after it all fell apart shows how God was with me every step of the way and how He had so beautifully taken care of me.

As if meeting my needs were not enough, I was given much more. The following highlights of events and travel opportunities chronicled far exceeded any expectation beyond providing the necessities that I could have ever dreamed.

Count it all joy . . . when you meet trials . . . for you know that the testing of your faith produces steadfastness. And let steadfastness have its full effect, that you may be perfect and complete, lacking in nothing. (James 1:2–4 ESV)

Again, God had given me more than my share.

John called when I had just made the arrangements to go to Ohio to the black mold doctor. I told him of my plans and that I needed to make another trip to Switzerland as soon as possible to see Bea. She had Parkinson's and had just had breast cancer surgery, and she wanted me to visit her. She claimed me as her cousin; we were related by my marriage to Richard Kelly. Her husband, Ed, was Kelly's cousin.

I was in Kelly's office in the courthouse one day while he was opening personal mail. A letter from an Ed Kelly posted from Switzerland read, "If you are the Richard Kelly who, as a child, lived in Clearwater with your grandmother . . ." Ed had sent this letter to every Richard Kelly in Florida he could find listed.

Kelly responded to Ed's letter but did not see him until he and Bea came to Washington for Sherri's wedding to Michael Hough in 1988. We had been invited many times to visit them in Switzerland and to their home in Spain. I had corresponded with them over the intervening twenty-seven years, but we had never met. "If ever there were a time for us to meet, it is now. Please come to Sherri's wedding," I had written them. They came, even though Ed was with an oxygen tank. We bonded as family. Bea and I shared the same birthday. Sadly, Ed died soon after their trip to Washington. I would have treasured more time with him.

Too much time had passed for Bea's affairs due to Ed's death not having been settled by her lawyer. This was causing her great anguish along with her health issues. She wanted my help. Her lawyer reluctantly gave me the responsibility of U.S.-related business when I offered to help during our visit to his office in Lausanne. Bea was a native of Switzerland, and Ed was in the United States Air Force when they met in the states. Bea was attending college in Alabama on a student-teacher arrangement.

Sometime later, Bea came to Washington and stayed with me for a month. I asked Bea what she would most like to do, as I had been so accustomed to doing for family and friends from home. I had heard requests of everything from seeing the White House and Congress in session to the Zoo to see the pandas. Bea wanted to meet Hillary Clinton. Luckily, the First Ladies Luncheon was scheduled during her visit, and her wish was fulfilled. She went home with a plate from the White House Dessert Collection marked First Lady's Luncheon, May 21, 1997.

Bea was accustomed to the privileges that came with being a major's wife in the military, and I had updated her pass to all bases. She arranged a luncheon at Andrews Air Force base and was given access to the room reserved for the president. Her stay in Washington lifted her spirits to a new high. She left with renewed hope for her life without Ed.

I returned to Washington from Ohio to get a message from John that he was going with me to Switzerland and had already made all the arrangements. What a blessing this was for me and for Bea. To see Bea and "to be traveling with John was as much as any mother's heart could stand," I wrote then. Sherri had visited Bea and

Ed in Switzerland, but they had only met John in Washington at Sherri's wedding to Michael.

John had reserved a car for us in Geneva on March 16, 2004. I would have been taking a train to Lausanne and then public transportation when visiting Bea in nearby Lutry and doing it alone. It would already be difficult enough because of my not speaking French.

We checked into a nice little bed-and-breakfast kind of hotel that John had booked. The *Le Rivage* was a picturesque place facing Lake Geneva and Evian, France, just across the lake. We then called to arrange a visit with Bea at the nursing home necessary for her convalescence following her surgery. She was overjoyed at seeing us.

John was a fearless driver. On Bea's good days we took her on nostalgic trips to places her family had lived and frequented, reliving memories of her childhood. We ate at what had been her mother's favorite restaurant and reminisced about times of being sent to their chalet in the Alps for fresh air believed to be good for a cold. Her father was a noted surgeon.

Special for me was visiting L'Abri, Francis Schaeffer's home, on our way to Gruyeres, a charming village of a medieval character, located near the top of the mountains. Lunch of raclette (two pounds of hot cheese with boiled potatoes), fondue (a pot of cheese with bread), and ice cream at Restaurant La Fleur de Lys was more than delicious; it was an experience. Why didn't Bea have a cholesterol problem?

John and I wanted to help Bea as much as possible while we were there. She suggested my calling her lawyer, Olivier Bourgeois. We called his office and reported our visit and offered help in any way possible. Bea expressed her concern about the lawyer's having made the nursing home, Chateau de la Rive, her permanent residence. She was looking forward to returning to her home in Lausanne.

John and I felt that our visit was the good medicine Bea needed. That was our intent, and she was very grateful. She was too generous with her gifts that trip and later.

The following is a paper I wrote for a class at American University:

Christmas 1992 fulfilled a lifelong dream to travel. Working for Middle Easterners, my daughter's marrying British, and my son's living in Idaho has given me three very diverse areas of the world to visit. Six weeks bridging December and January took me to Dubai in the United Arab Emirates, Wappenham near Towcester in England, and Coeur d'Alene, Idaho, in the states. After living most of my adult life with a politician who believed and had published that his wife should not travel at the public's expense, my time had come.

I flew British Airways via London to Dubai on December 5, by invitation to attend the wedding of Haifa to Emad from Kuwait. All arrangements had been made for me, visa secured, and ticket in hand. Family members met me at the Dubai airport upon my arrival at two in the morning after a journey that had taken me half way around the world. What was to be an Arabian fairy tale had begun.

By Arab standards, Haifa and Emad's wedding was a small one—even so, there were thousands of guests. The invitation to the wedding came from the mothers of the bride and groom, as was the custom. I was to learn that the wedding was a four-day event, and the appropriate wedding gift was gold. The first day of the wedding was in Kuwait with the groom's family.

The men were received for dinner separately for the big formal night in the Golf Garden of the Hyatt Regency overlooking the Persian Gulf. The thousands of elegantly attired women dined and partied in the hotel ballroom prepared for the occasion in the style of "Arabian Nights." Only a few men of the immediate family of the bride and groom were allowed to penetrate the colorful harem-like scene of beautiful women who danced to Arabian music down a lengthy runway to greet the bride and groom seated on their imposing throne.

I was escorted down the runway and sat on the throne with the bride and groom for a photo. The father of the bride then invited me to meet the few men with him in a lower box to the right of the stage. I needed some help in getting down and even more in getting back out. When I asked what to wear when this invitation came, I was told to just send measurements. All of my clothes needed were made for me. The morning after I arrived in Dubai my assigned driver took me for final fittings. The dress for this evening was long, tight, and elegant. Even gold jewelry was provided and was later given to me.

The following evening was a reception and fabulous dinner in Arabian tents on Jebel Ali. Waiters were in Arabian robes and fez serving guests seated on sumptuous pillows. Malcolm Forbes's event could not have been better. The bride with the backdrop of a full moon, the biggest I have ever seen, arrived on the back of a camel. Guests were entertained by dancers to Arabian music until the morning hours.

Several family members invited the wedding guests for luncheons and dinners that provided the perfect opportunities to see a variety of homes in Dubai and experience their culture and customs. One invitation was to the new home of Samia, sister of the bride, and her husband, Tariq. The furnishings of this home had been chosen at the Design Center in Washington and had arrived just in time to entertain wedding guests. The relatively new homes would appear from the air to be postage stamps in the desert. The walled gardens around the homes were beautifully landscaped; outside the walls was desert sand.

After the wedding and the many related events that filled two weeks in the United Arab Emirates, the Arabian fairy-tale portion of my journey had come to an end. Haifa may have been the bride, but I was made to feel a queen!

The first class ticket allowed a stopover of three days in England to visit Sherri, Michael, and the boys. To travel in England is like experiencing a living, illustrated history book. You can ponder over the ancient mystery of Stonehenge, relive the days of Roman Britain while walking through an excavated villa, and hear the linguistic influence of languages such as Celtic, Norse, and Norman in words and place names. The very smallness of the landmass of England makes it possible to see a lot in a comparatively short time.

Michael's driver met me at Heathrow Airport and drove me to Victoria Station to catch the train to Milton Keynes in the country, a one-hour journey. Sherri and my newest grandson at that time, Edward, born November 4, and Harry, then two, met the train. We then drove the twenty minutes to their three-hundred-year-old Georgian country house in a very small village right out of Charles Dickens.

After a short rest to recover from jet lag, Sherri and I took the boys to the village community center where the small children gathered to meet Santa. Seeing Harry meet Santa for the first time was a treasured moment. Back home, the customary afternoon tea was enjoyed and provided time to get to know Edward. The decorations were then taken out of storage, greenery was cut for garlands, and Harry and I had special time together decorating the house for Christmas. He was my best helper. Fire in the fireplaces, the aroma of good food cooking, sounds of music, and family, especially grandchildren, were the makings of a warm and wonderful visit.

I arrived back in Washington, D.C., on the twenty-first of December, unpacked desert clothes, added warmer clothes, and left the following day for Idaho to be with John and his family for Christmas. My flight arrived at the Spokane, Washington, airport where John and my granddaughter, Kalan (two), met the plane.

Most of Idaho, in spite of its northern location, has a milder climate than Great Plains states in the same latitude. Winds from the Pacific Ocean warmed the state, and mountains protect it from cold northern winds during the winter. However, that was not to be my experience that visit. The snowdrifts covered the barn. John wore snowshoes that he had worn in Alaska to get over the drifts to feed the horses.

John's work in law enforcement and Kathy's at the hospital required their services even though the highways were closed. A four-wheel vehicle made their reporting to work possible. The opportunity to have Kalan home alone was more than I had hoped. The soup was on for the day, and we were enjoying breakfast together when smoke from the stove was filling the room. Every attempt at adjusting the damper failed. The smoke alarm went off, and an emergency call to John brought help from neighbors and the fire department. Kalan was taken across the road to neighbors for safety. The firemen determined that the snowdrifts were so fierce that the chimney had been iced over, and the smoke backed into the house. When John told his superior that his mother was home alone with his baby and the fire department on its way, he was told to go home.

The remainder of our visit was uneventful by comparison. Being snowed in, we enjoyed a lot of togetherness that would not have happened had the weather been different.

There were tea parties with Kalan, reading, listening to music, telling stories, and cooking for John all of the foods he enjoyed and remembered eating as a child so that his child could have the same memories. This reminded me of a pillow that I had seen, "Mothers build memories."

We truly had a "white Christmas." This was the second Christmas that John had planned a horse-drawn sleigh ride for me—the first, not enough snow—the second, too much snow! The weather finally cleared enough for me to be taken to the airport for my return trip home.

Going from the Middle Eastern desert to the blizzards of Idaho in one trip satisfied temporarily the dream to travel. Since an Arabian fairy tale was possible, why not dream of the ultimate trip around the world!

Many trips followed, but most were to England, especially with the births of four grandchildren there—Harry, Edward, Ellie, and Georgia.

———————————

Mary Glynn asked what I had planned to celebrate the upcoming centennial year 2000. Her suggestion: Oberammergau to the *Passion Play*.

During the Thirty Years' War, the deadly and contagious disease known as the Black Plague broke out in Germany. Before it ran its course, it struck down one in every three persons throughout Europe and left in its wake untold misery, panic, and hunger. It reached everywhere, even to sailors out at sea who had not been to port in many months. Nowhere could safety or escape be found from this dreadful disease. But one little village in the south of Germany was spared: Oberammergau.

The townspeople of Oberammergau had made a vow that if they were spared they would give a play of the life of Christ every ten years. The fact that they were saved is one of the most amazing mysteries in history.

Thus, the first *Passion Play* took place in 1634. Originally it was a small production, performed in a meadow by villagers and local peasants. Throughout the years, however, Oberammergau has produced several gifted poets who have set the *Play* to verse as well as lengthen it, until it achieved its present form as an artistic masterwork. To qualify as actors, the performers must be natives of the town, persons of high moral and ethical principles and amateur—rather than professional—actors. It is a great honor to be chosen to play the part of Christ. The beautiful costumes are made by local villagers and the actors' long hair is natural (no wigs), as they begin to grow their hair and beards a year or more in advance to prepare for the play.

For the people of this village, the *Play* is a labor of love. The hundreds of actors involved receive no reimbursement for their time and devotion to the exhausting performances (seven hours a day, four days a week from May until October). Although the widespread fame of the *Passion Play* and international tourism have brought audiences from all over the world, the complete sincerity of the Oberammergauers has never been dimmed. Their vow is still the most important thing in their lives, and it is with great pride that they were even then already preparing for the *Passion Play* 2010.

We began our trip in Munich, then to Oberammergau, and on to Germany's Romantic Road. Another photo album was made of this trip.

Sherri joined us from England, Lucia and French Boone from Washington, D.C., several from Birmingham, Alabama, making about a dozen friends celebrating the turn of a new century in the best kind of way.

On the morning of September 11, 2001, we were up early at John's in Post Falls, Idaho, almost ready to leave for Spokane, Washington, to catch my early flight back to Washington, D.C. John just happened to turn on the television to learn that one of the World Trade Center towers had been hit by an airplane. We could not believe what we were seeing or hearing. As we were watching, the second tower was hit. As a result, all flights were cancelled across the country. The flights in the air from Spokane were diverted to Canada. My visit to John was extended to a three-week visit.

Looking out the window of the plane on my return flight to Washington as we approached National Airport, I could see the damage to the Pentagon.

There were a series of four coordinated terrorist attacks by the Islamic terrorist group al-Qaeda on the U.S. in New York City and the Washington, D.C., metropolitan area that killed 2,996 people and caused at least $10 billion in property and infrastructure damage.

Four passenger airliners were hijacked by nineteen terrorists to be flown into buildings in suicide attacks. Two of the planes, American Airlines Flight 11 and United Airlines Flight 175, were crashed into the north and south towers, respectively, of the World Trade Center complex in New York City. Within two hours, both 110-story towers collapsed with debris, and the resulting fires caused partial or complete collapse of all other buildings in the WTC complex. A third plane, American Airlines Flight 77, was crashed into the Pentagon (the headquarters of the United States Department of Defense), leading to a partial collapse in its western side. The fourth plane, United Airlines Flight 93, was targeted at

Washington, D.C., but crashed into a field near Shanksville, Pennsylvania, after its passengers tried to overcome the hijackers. In total, 2,996 people died in the attacks, including the 227 civilians and nineteen hijackers aboard the four planes. It was the deadliest incident for firefighters and law enforcement officers in the history of the United States, with 343 and seventy-two killed, respectively.

Because of these attacks, our world as we knew it had changed forever.

Gloria and Dennis Saunders, from Columbia, Maryland, became very special friends when we met in August, 1988. Gloria loves the Lord with a passion. Whenever you meet this note in a person, you feel that person is after God's own heart.

Steve O'Brien was marrying Eileen Deymier. Rather than have me stay in a hotel with the other guests, they had arranged for me to stay with the Saunders, who lived next door to Eileen. I got to know their son and daughter, Ryan and Robin, even going with Robin and her mother shopping for her wedding dress. We shared many good times together. Robin has included me in some very special family events.

Early on in 2002, the following came from Robin and Matt, her husband:

> This June heralds a trio of epochal events for our family, and we would be delighted if you would join us for a related series of special celebrations in and around the great city of Florence, Italy, during the weekend of the 14th. Formal invitations will be sent shortly with additional details, but please hold the dates and commence preparations!

> On the evening of June 14, we invite you to celebrate the 40th birthday of Robin at the Palazzo Corsini situated on the river Arno. This magnificent Renaissance palace was the home of the noble Corsini family. Festivities will include a formal dinner accompanied by a serenade from three tenors, followed by dancing under the stars.

Dress was black tie, evening gowns for ladies. We were taken to the palace in horse-drawn carriages. People lined the streets to watch us as if we were movie stars.

We have left all day of Saturday free to allow for relaxing, shopping, and sightseeing. However, on Saturday evening, the pace quickens as we step back in time to fifteenth-century Florence to celebrate our tenth wedding anniversary. For this event, we will be hosting a costumed Renaissance ball in the magnificent Castello di Vincigliata, located above the hills of Fiesole, about five miles from Florence.

The Renaissance Costume Ball is built around the story of Lorenzo de' Medici, the master of Florence during the high point of the Florentine Renaissance. With your participation—along with the musicians, jugglers, fire eaters and other entertainers that formed the tapestry of the Renaissance Period—we hope to recreate the period balls held by the Medici family.

We were asked to send our measurements for the preparation of the Renaissance ball. The horses were even in costume when we arrived at the castle for the ball.

> On Sunday, we are delighted to invite you to attend the christening of our girls, Savannah and Ella, in Florence. The christening will be followed by a lunch at the Gardens of Corsini, also located in the heart of Florence. All children are welcome to the events of this day.
>
> Traveling to Florence: For those of you flying in from the U.S. or Asia, we would recommend arriving on Thursday to mitigate the jet lag. For anyone arriving by boat, the local ports are Viareggio and Livorno. The closest airports are clearly Florence, Pisa, Rome, and Milan.

Hollywood would have been pleased with this production, and I was privileged and grateful for having been included.

One of Mary Glynn's friends had just moved to Washington, and Mary Glynn had asked if I would see her from time to time. Martha and I were having dinner one evening before attending a play at the Kennedy Center when I mentioned that I had never gotten so many interesting invitations. Martha was a very social person and wanted to know more. When I named Robin's parties in Florence, Italy, she said, "Go, and I'll go with you." Gloria called for my response and told me that I would be seated with the family. It was then that I mentioned Martha's interest. She went with me to Italy and is still talking about this one as being one of the best.

Much was reported in the tabloids about how much Robin spent on "giving herself a birthday party." Robin is a most unusual young woman who had been very successful and so generously shares the rewards with her family and friends.

Robin is a proud graduate of Florida State University who has done very well. FSU is equally as proud of her and has written about her success.

This trip to Italy became even more exciting when we were invited to Rome. Jim Nicholson had just been sworn in as ambassador to the Vatican, and he and his wife, Suzanne, had invited me to join their family for the swearing in ceremony at the State Department. Suzanne was in our Friday Group at Joanne's, and she and I had painted together. She was a beautifully trained artist in mostly watercolors. The Christmas cards of her paintings have been saved. Suzanne suggested at that time that I come to Rome and paint with her. Never in my wildest dreams did I think this could ever happen.

After the parties were over in Florence, we took the train to Rome. I had called Suzanne, and she invited me and my guest to stay at the U.S. Embassy to the Holy See. A dinner party was given for us and other guests, and tours were arranged for us to see the best of Rome. We enjoyed being with the Nicholsons and appreciated their hospitality. They represented our country well. Going to Rome became the frosting on the cake of our trip to Italy.

Any opportunity to be with grandchildren was treasured. "Edward's Visit with Grammy, May 29–June 15, 2004" (joined by Mummy, Ellie and Georgia for the second week) is from the album of this trip. Harry was visiting Uncle John and his family and "Bows and Arrows" Grandpa Kelly in Idaho and Montana. This special trip to Washington, D.C., was a getaway from the Island during the G-8 Summit hosted by President Bush on Sea Island.

Edward and I had special time together the first week, including Mr. and Mrs. Boone's (Lucia and French) treating us to a birthday brunch/dance cruise on the Potomac aboard the Odyssey celebrating my birthday on May 30, visiting the International Spy Museum, the Smithsonian Einstein Planetarium at the National Air and Space Museum, the Sports Arena, the dedication of the National World War II Memorial, and we even took a photo of the memorial from the top of the Washington Monument. Edward was so handsome, dressed in his blue blazer and tie, when we attended a performance of *Children of Eden* at Ford's Theatre. He thought himself overly dressed when a busload of students dressed in shorts and flip flops arrived. I assured him that he was more appropriately dressed.

When Sherri and the girls arrived for the second week, we continued our touring with the Bureau of Engraving and Printing, Panda Mania, Washington Monument, Jefferson Memorial, Lincoln Memorial, Franklin Delano Roosevelt Memorial, Corcoran Gallery of Art, Smithsonian, National Museum of Natural History, Johnson IMAX Theatre, Arlington National Cemetery, President John F. Kennedy's grave, and Robert F. Kennedy's grave; and we witnessed the changing of the guard at the Tomb of the Unknown Soldier. All of this sounds exhausting, but it was fun.

While at Arlington Cemetery, I met Dr. Mitchell Jones for the first time. He had also left the Island because of the G-8 Summit and was with his mother and two sons, Henry and Will. We invited them to Prospect House. I thought him to be very nice and suggested to Sherri, since he was a single parent, that it would be nice to invite them for a swim. Her response was "Mom, I'm not helping any man." She had been burned by her former marriage. On November 2006, Mitchell became her husband.

The biggest and saddest happening of all was "Ronald Reagan Dies." Tens of thousands approached the Capitol in the spirit of tribute. We were on the front line, and I photographed the caisson carrying his coffin as it came by on Pennsylvania Avenue—it was the same caisson that carried President Lincoln's body.

After his service at Washington National Cathedral, Ronald Reagan's flag-draped coffin was carried by members of the U.S. armed forces past his widow and children to be taken to his Presidential Library and Museum in Simi Valley, California, for burial.

We toured the Washington National Cathedral the next day.

A friend, who was an art teacher at the Corcoran, called to tell me that her students had not shown up for class that day because of the heavy snow. That if I were willing to risk going out in the bad weather, come to her and she promised I would leave with a painting. She knew of my interest in art and had included me from time to time on her class tours, especially to the National Museum of Art and the Corcoran. Pat Hutchens and I became even closer friends on that snowy day and enjoyed painting together. I'm thankful for her friendship and the tutelage under her, and especially for inspiring me to paint. She wrote, "You have the right spirit, the right touch, the right everything. I look forward to many years of friendship and art, Lord willing!"

I was excited to tell John about my painting. His response was "Mom, this is no surprise. You have always sketched from my earliest memories." Drawings in my design work had never been considered art.

Soon after this first effort at painting with Pat, I went to Sherri's in England to help with decorating her new home, Showsley. I had asked where she wanted me to begin in this house with twenty-two rooms. She wanted the larder done first to store her food. Harry wanted to help. While I'm cleaning and painting, I gave him paints and taped a rectangular frame on the wall for his painting. His painting was priceless.

This wonderful 1600s country house was located in hunt country, and I suggested our going to London and look for a reproduction of George Stubb's famous *Hound* painting for her family room. We were successful in finding one but it was much too small and too costly -- $4,000 for a small reproduction was not what we had in mind. I suggested that I copy my version of the painting and make it the right size. "Ahhh, Mom" was the response as only Sherri can say it, as if I could not do it. At an Open House at Christmas, a titled Lady, very regal in her dress with a full-feathered collar, reeked, "My gaaaaad, you have a George Stubbs!" It must have passed the test; she wanted me to paint one for her.

More than seventy paintings were painted for that house in England. If not good, I'm fast. Even a mural was painted on the wall of the children's sitting room. The children watched and excitedly voiced their choices. Harry wanted to be in a rocket going to the moon, Edward wanted to be on a tractor bailing hay, Ellie wanted to be in a hot air balloon, and Georgia was a baby riding with Harry. Now, put all of that together in a painting! Among the more unusual for them was a three-panel stage for a puppet show, reversible to a lemonade stand. They loved it, and the boys loved their farms painted for them from Santa. Kalan and Paige had walls in their bedrooms done with scenes from fairy tales.

Many other paintings are in Tanzania, Dubai, Spain, Switzerland, London, and others scattered across the U.S. All of this makes me sound like an artist, but I just have a love of painting.

_____

Included in my dreams of retirement was going to France to paint, walking on the beach barefooted eating ice cream cones, and going on a cruise with my grandchildren.

On September 2006, my dream of going to the south of France to paint was fulfilled. I had attended an art exhibit of Connie Winters' paintings at the Anderson Gallery on St. Simons Island. Sherri mentioned to Mary Anderson that I loved to paint, and she suggested that I sign up for "Connie Winters' Painting Holiday in France, September 13–23." Imagine signing on with Connie Winters and fourteen women who were strangers to me to explore and paint the lush Dordogne region of France.

The workshop was held in Hotel Perigord Vert in Brantome, France, in a village on an island created by a mill stream on the river Dronne. It had just enough rooms to accommodate our group. The entire hotel was ours. A young couple owned the hotel, and the husband was an excellent chef. Gardens and parks surrounding much of the town and bridges created a painter's dream layout. We had permission to paint throughout the village.

From my photo album of this trip, "Behold, how good and how pleasant it is for brethren to dwell together in unity" (Psalm 133:1). This was by far the friendliest and most interesting group of women one could ever have hoped to share a trip. I would love to do it all over again with them. It was such a well-organized trip that included painting, excursions, good food, and fellowship.

Two days after returning to the Island from France on September 2006, I left for Washington to attend an autumn lunch on the twenty-seventh to celebrate Joanne's seventieth birthday at the Cedars. It was given by her daughters, Stacy, Susan, Judith, and Jennifer, "along with the thoughtful patronage of our dad," Jack. This was a gathering of family and friends made extra special by a reunion of former Friday Group members who had come from all over the country to celebrate with the Kemps.

Joanne and I had talked about attending the First Lady's Luncheon honoring Laura Bush being held on May 10, 2007. Sherri had never attended one of these luncheons, and I asked if she were interested. She appreciated this opportunity to be with her godchild, Meagan, and to enjoy this special occasion with friends Joanne and I had invited to share our table.

On October 2010, another travel opportunity came from my neighbors in the Gates, Dale and Paul Cronin. I had recouped well enough after my surgery in 2008 to continue my love of travel. They had made reservations for a Silversea cruise on the Silver Cloud going to Greece and the Greek Isles.

One of my Washington children, Irene, had visited me in Idaho the summer after my surgery. She rented a car thinking a road trip would be good for me. We went to Seattle, stopping at intervals along the way as necessary for my leg, and stayed at a hotel that extended over the water. Next door we could see cruise ships waiting to depart and thought about getting aboard. We agreed to look into taking a cruise together at a later date.

When the invitation came from Dale and Paul, I contacted Irene with the details and asked if this would work for her. We were all aboard!

This trip became the one that would be hard to repeat. Irene was the perfect partner for this trip. Others on the cruise wanted to join us in having such a great time. Friends we met on the cruise wrote:

> Our cruise was so wonderful and meeting you (Dale, Paul, Irene, and Loraine) was one of the best aspects of our trip. Our excursions were made more interesting when you were with us, and our evenings were most definitely enlivened in your company. We had a lot of fun as evidenced by how the time flew by. We certainly hope to cruise with you again—a good way to be assured of a great time!

Retirement allowed more time to play bridge. The Bridge Club with Margaret Altman, a dear friend as our teacher, broadened my circle of friends even more. My love of travel had also included a couple of bridge cruises with Audrey Grant, who had established an international reputation in the field of bridge education.

I was not getting any younger and still with the dream of taking the grandchildren on a cruise. Harry was most interested, and we talked about destinations with a travel agent. Alaska was the choice. An invitation was put out to the children and grandchildren to reserve the date.

Sherri's children had traveled extensively with their dad but had never been on a cruise, except Georgia. Sherri had gone with her on a school trip cruise on a very large ship and had shared a cabin with only a porthole. I wanted this one to be better.

We arranged to meet, and our journey began on July 24, 2012, with a couple of days at the Loden Hotel in Vancouver before boarding our ship. We enjoyed everything Vancouver had to offer plus Victoria Island and Butchart Gardens, a world renowned fifty-acre estate which included a sunken garden lake, a Japanese garden, a formal Italian garden, and a charming English rose garden.

Silversea's highly personalized style of travel was readily apparent in the choices offered in your suite. Firm or soft mattress? Queen or twin bed?

Bvlgari or Ferragamo toiletries? We were told that this was our own private sanctuary so customize it as we please. And all of our suites featured private verandas so that we could breathe in the fresh ocean air by merely stepping outside our door. Every suite included a butler who was available to take care of all the details because we had better things to do on vacation.

We enjoyed this beautiful ship with 382 guests, distinguished by a special brand of Italian warmth and European sophistication, the freedom and flexibility of an all-inclusive lifestyle, the exquisite cuisine served in its restaurants, and of course, our spacious suites crowned by all the pampering of the experienced butler.

Our excursions included fishing, kayaking, taking a zip line expedition directly above glacially fed waterfalls, a helicopter ride to the top of Mendenhall Glacier to dog sled. Yes, I did it! And there was more fishing and seeing the whales!

This was a wonder-filled cruise that satisfied another dream of sharing something wonderful and extraordinary with my family in the hopes of building warm memories for the years to come. Regrettably, all did not participate.

Soon after the Alaskan cruise I had cause to be concerned about my cancer having returned, enough so that I made an appointment with the surgeon Dr. Reintgen in Tampa. Dr. Cavalier locally had seen the growth and wanted to biopsy it, but instructions from Dr. Reintgen included no one to cut on this leg for fear of infection.

Edward, my grandson, drove me to Tampa, and Dr. Reintgen was certain enough that the cancer had returned and that biopsying the spot was the only recourse to be sure. We talked about my choices: do nothing or try perfusion again. Knowing that I could not survive that surgery again having come close to not surviving the first one, I returned home to await the report of the biopsy. I was at peace with any outcome.

Dr. Reintgen called me directly to ask if I wanted good news. He reported the spot was scar tissue from the former surgery. Dale was with me when I received the call and shouted, "Let's celebrate.

Go with me and Paul on a river cruise in Germany."
I thanked God—then would have said "yes" to
almost anything.

Elizabeth, a neighbor, was my partner for this cruise
with the Cronins, on November 30–December
10, 2012. Jacksonville, Atlanta, Amsterdam,
and Cologne began our fun and fascinating
exploration of a treasured European holiday
tradition, the wonderful Christmas markets of
Germany and France along the Rhine. Our eight-
day voyage on the riverboat, Swiss Sapphire,
showcased a variety of German markets in
Aachen, Rudesheim, Heidelberg, and Baden-
Baden, as well as French markets in Strasbourg,
Riquewihr and Colmar. This was river travel at its
best, with good friends creating more memories
to last a lifetime. Baden-Baden was my favorite,
and I was to learn that my father's family had
come from there.

On April 2013, Robin gave her parents, Gloria
and Dennis, who were high school sweethearts,
a combined seventieth birthday party and
invited every member of her family. I was the only

non-family member invited on an all-expense paid trip to Barbados staying at Mullins Mill.

Mullins Mill was a home of unique character nestled on eight acres of landscaped grounds. The main house was constructed around a seventeenth-century sugar mill. The grounds offered privacy there and the two adjoining guest cottages. A cozy gazebo on the cliff side had sweeping views of the coastline, and the property had a ridge side infinity swimming pool with cabana and separate Jacuzzi located a short walk through the tropical gardens (about a hundred yards) south of the main house. East of the main house were a tennis court, a garden, and an orchard. Mullins Mill was the ideal choice for families—two bedrooms were located in the main house (one at the top of the mill), two in the adjoining cliff cottage, and two more in the guest cottage on the grounds. Robin and I shared the guest cottage. A spacious sitting/dining veranda overlooked the gardens and cliff side gazebo and offered fantastic ocean views.

Mullins Mill was fully staffed, including a chef and a beautiful boat with the captain available to us at all times.

May 2013: It is hard to believe that five years had passed since that eightieth birthday party Sherri gave for me and my many friends and God's gift of five years of a full life since my cancer surgery. Friends were already asking what Sherri was doing for my eighty-fifth and if they could be included. My thought was to give back.

As a thank you for the eightieth birthday party, I took Sherri to Paris to celebrate my eighty-fifth birthday. She had been to Paris before, but this was my first trip. We had a slow and disappointing start when the weather delayed our flight out of JFK in New York by twenty-four hours, but we made up for it shopping in Manhattan. All was forgiven when we arrived at Hotel Lutetia located near Bon Marché and began our holiday in Paris.

We benefited from the arranged excursions minibus tour that allowed us to see up front and personal all of the highlights of Paris without standing in line. We were taken to the underground parking at the Louvre and immediately were given a guided tour, which included seeing the *Mona Lisa* and so much more. Our lunch was aboard a luxurious river boat with entertainment while cruising the Seine River. I had just read *The Paris Wife* by Ernest Hemingway, and it was a treat to see where he and his wife lived at that time. A friend, Margaret Lewis, was then living in Paris, and she and her family contributed much in making our visit to Paris memorable.

John and I had gone to Switzerland together; now I have had a one-on-one trip with Sherri to Paris. My bucket list was being satisfied.

Conclusion

But we are not of those who shrink back
and are destroyed, but of those who
believe and are saved. (Hebrews 10:39)

My husband was being tried again in 1969, this time in his own courtroom. My mother was dying of cancer, and at the same time I was director of a Mothers Weekend Conference, Presbyterian Conference Center, in Lake Placid, Florida. As I was leaving our home on my way to the courthouse in Dade City to be with my husband, I stopped at the bottom of the hill to look in the back seat to see Jesus. In a most reassuring voice, he said, "I am with you." He has been true to his promise and has been my sufficiency. Oswald Chambers has written, "When once you have seen Jesus, you can never be the same."

As I look back on my journey thus far, I can see that days of extreme weakness had been some of my most precious times. "Life isn't about how to survive the storm but how to dance in the rain." Memories of those days were richly interwoven with golden strands of his intimate Presence. *He gives us life as we overcome.*

My desires for the remaining years are to keep the faith, enjoy family and friends, and finish my life strong. Relationships are vital, and God has richly blessed me. We all need encouragement, prayer, someone who will really listen to what we have to say and who will contribute in making us the person God wants us to be.

When my time comes to be taken to Glory, I hope to be greeted there by the many people to whom I had told about his Grace and Love.

49931433R00181